# Coppola

## A Pediatric Surgeon in Iraq

*Dr. Chris Coppola*

NTI UPSTREAM  CHICAGO 2009

For a complete list of our publications, please write to:

NTI Upstream
180 North Michigan Avenue
Suite 700
Chicago, Illinois 60601

Phone: 877-500-5726
Fax: 312-726-4021

www.coppolathebook.com
www.ntiupstream.com

The names and details concerning some individuals in *Coppola: A Pediatric Surgeon in Iraq* have been changed. Dates of certain events have been altered.

Grateful acknowledgement is made to the American Medical Association for permission to reprint portions of "Children Treated at an Expeditionary Military Hospital in Balad" by Lt. Col. Christopher P. Coppola, Maj. Brian E. Leininger, Lt. Col. Todd E. Rasmussen, and Col. David L. Smith (*Archives of Pediatric and Adolescent Medicine* 2006; Vol. 160: pgs 972-976). Copyright © 2006 American Medical Association. All rights reserved.

Extra-Corporeal Membrane Oxygenation pediatric life support cart sketch previously published in "A 22-year experience in global transport extracorporeal membrane oxygenation" by Christopher P. Coppola, Melissa Tyree, Karen Larry, Robert DiGeronimo (*Journal of Pediatric Surgery* 2008; Vol. 43, Issue 1: pgs 46-52). Copyright © 2008 Elsevier. Reprinted with permission.

All photos and sketches by Lt. Col. Christopher P. Coppola, except Jeep photo (152), front cover photo, and author photograph on rear cover by NTI Upstream.

Cover design by Jennifer Carrow
Cover photo by Billy Gene
Edited by Jeff Link

Printed in the United States of America

First Printing: February 2010

ISBN-13: 978-0-9840531-1-7

Library of Congress Number 2009933155

*Dear sweet Meredith, every day by your side amazes me that I can be so lucky. Ti Amo.*

*With malice toward none, with charity for all, with firmness in the right as God gives us to see the right, let us strive on to finish the work we are in, to bind up the nation's wounds, to care for him who shall have borne the battle and for his widow and his orphan, to do all which may achieve and cherish a just and lasting peace among ourselves and with all nations.*

— ABRAHAM LINCOLN
*Second Inaugural Address*
*March 4, 1865*

# Contents

# Foreword

- Guy Raz, NPR Correspondent

THE US MILITARY sees itself as an apolitical institution. The men and women who make up its ranks follow the guidance and orders of their civilian leaders—no matter the ideology behind that guidance.

But plumb the surface and you'll find that, on a personal level, there are ideological differences right up and down the chain of command. I once met an officer in Iraq who described his colleagues, half tongue-in-cheek, as "conservative socialists."

"We like strong leaders, we are motivated by love of country and the pursuit of freedom," he said. "Many of us are religious and deeply committed to the 'American' way of life. And yet," he added with a smile, "the Army is one of the last great bastions in America where you'll find a cradle-to-grave, socialist-style, welfare safety net."

The wisdom of invading and then occupying Iraq is constantly under debate among the men and women sent to carry out the mission. There are differences—strong differences—of opinion. But what unites all of these Americans is a commitment to serve—service even in the pursuit of a policy they might personally question.

These citizen-soldiers, sailors, airmen and marines are motivated by factors such as love of country, sacrifice, honor, sometimes revenge for what happened on 9-11, even ideology. But for some of these men and women, these factors are deeply overshadowed by something greater: saving lives. And it is among this medical core where I most experienced the greatness, humility, empathy, and courage of our armed forces. They are the life-givers and the life-savers—the doctors, nurses, and medical technicians who serve to save.

I remember sitting outside in the warm autumn air of Bagram Air Base at night, talking about the merits of going to war in Iraq with a group of medevac pilots from Ft. Campbell, Kentucky. Some of the soldiers felt deeply committed to the stated ideology behind the war—to liberate Iraq from tyranny, as they saw it. Others believed the civilian leaders who brought them here had failed—even lied. And yet every single soldier in that unit—everyone—they were all highly motivated by what they did. "We save lives," a young 2nd Lieutenant from Virginia told me. "That's it. Iraqi, American, soldier, marine, airmen, sailor, civilian, child, woman, terrorist, insurgent. All of them. We scrape their half-dead bodies from the battlefield and rush them to the ER where most of them will be given their lives back."

The history of warfare has not been generous to soldiers wounded on the battlefield. In the First World War, a wounded infantryman faced an 80 percent chance of dying. By World War II, that number reached 60 percent. In Vietnam, one out of three wounded never made it. But in Iraq, nearly 97 percent of troops injured in the field have survived. It's an unprecedented rate of survival and a statistic that owes much to the work of military doctors like Christopher Coppola.

I first met Dr. Coppola a few hours after I was released

from temporary detention at the Balad Air Base medical center. It was a bureaucratic error. I had followed a wounded soldier off a medevac helicopter and into the ER. My microphone was recording the dramatic moments—triage, assessment, emergency intervention. I had already spent a few weeks sleeping rough at the base, following the rescuers. My aim was to produce a long-form radio documentary chronicling the extraordinary work of US military medics in Iraq. My scraggly, unshaven face and disheveled hair caught the attention of a young Air Force public affairs officer. She hadn't expected my arrival. I was whisked away by a couple of tough-looking, heavily armed security contractors who demanded my audio. After several hours of back-and-forth, the public affairs crew realized that it was a mix-up. But I was frustrated, nevertheless. I lost several precious hours of recording time—audio that illustrated the heroism, grace and professionalism of the military's medical corps.

It was then I met a tall, wiry, and soft-spoken Lieutenant Colonel who introduced himself as "Chris." He wanted to apologize for the mix-up. But more importantly, he wanted to take me into the OR where a young Iraqi girl—barely six years old—was recovering from a shrapnel wound to her stomach. Dr. Coppola had just finished cleaning out the wound and the girl was recovering—soon to head to the intensive care unit.

"It's a sad fact that surgery has advanced and benefits from all the tragedies and trials of war," he told me.

On a typical day—particularly during the most violent periods in Iraq—a single patient might arrive with a destroyed eye, shrapnel embedded in his body, a massive chest wound and missing limbs. Chris and the doctors who worked there said the intensity of a week at the Air Force Theater hospital at Balad Air Base was equivalent to a year at a busy trauma center in the United States.

Virtually all of the military doctors who rotate in and out of the hospital at Balad for several months at a time come voluntarily. Like Chris, they are among the finest surgeons and physicians in the United States—men and women who could have pursued a lucrative career in the private sector.

My time at the theater hospital happened to coincide with a visit by the Admiral Michael Mullen, chairman of the Joint Chiefs of Staff. I watched as his entourage flew through the facility to visit wounded troops and praise the docs who saved their lives. "You are all heroes," Mullen said in brief remarks to a gathered audience in the ER.

Later that evening, I joined a group of doctors on the roof of the hospital as we sucked down cans of non-alcoholic beer. I asked Chris about Mullen's use of the word "hero."

"Have you been able to assimilate that notion that you're a hero?" I asked.

"We're not heroes," Chris whispered as we watched tracer fire in the distant black sky. "I'm uncomfortable with that word," he said. "We are trained to save lives. That's not heroism. That's what we do."

# Coppola

## A Pediatric Surgeon
## in Iraq

# First Tour
## January 2005 – May 2005

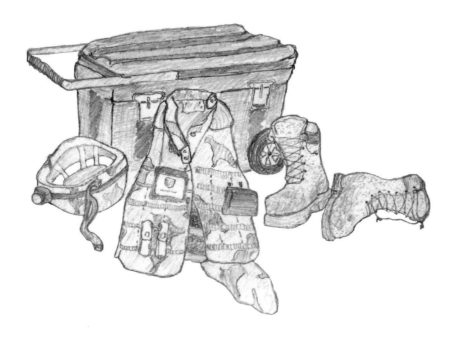

**DEPARTMENT OF THE AIR FORCE**
HEADQUARTERS UNITED STATES AIR FORCE RECRUITING SERVICE (ATC)
RANDOLPH AIR FORCE BASE, TX 78150 −5421

REPLY TO
ATTN OF: RSHM

13 Mar 90

SUBJECT: Appointment as a Reserve of the Air Force

TO: Second Lieutenant Christopher Paul Coppola,     FV, ResAF (MSC)
Post Office Box 615, Brown University
Providence RI 02912             HPSP/MED 94    AFSC: 9021

1. The Secretary of the Air Force has directed me to inform you that, by direction of the President, you are tendered an indefinite term appointment as a Reserve of the Air Force. Rank and service number are shown in the address above. Appointment is effective on date of acceptance.

2. Request you execute and return the Oath of Office at once. This action constitutes acceptance of your appointment and no other evidence is required. If you are unable to accept this appointment, return this letter with your statement of declination. Failure to respond to this tender of appointment within a reasonable time will result in cancellation.

3. You will not perform the duties of an officer under this appointment until specifically ordered by competent authority.

4. Authority for this appointment is 10 U.S.C. 593 and AFR 36-15.

*E. Edward Maxwell*
E. EDWARD MAXWELL, Major, USAF, BSC
Chief, Medical Recruiting Division
Directorate of Health Professions

AIR FORCE—A GREAT WAY OF LIFE

# Combat Landing

I WEAR my desert camouflage uniform, the creases still crisp from the alteration and pressing shop where my medical unit insignia and major's rank were sewn on. My matching eight-point Marine-style cap is stuffed in the right cargo pocket of my pants. Besides extra uniforms I have ballistic armor, a Kevlar helmet, a gas mask, and a chemical exposure suit, all of it packed in my trunk in the back of a minivan taxi.

I don't know what sort of a war I am heading into. It seems melodramatic to even consider, but I wonder if this will be the last time I ever see my wife. War isn't anything I would ever choose. I am a pediatric surgeon, and my work is correcting birth defects and helping children who need emergency surgery. Now I'm being sent to Iraq as a trauma surgeon to take care of troops injured in the war. I don't want to go. But I gave my word to serve in 1990 when I accepted a medical school scholarship from the military during my senior year at Brown—and I will keep my word.

Along the staging facility at Lackland Air Force Base, airmen in stateside green-camouflage uniforms are walking through the crowd with clipboards. I unload from the taxi, sign in, and drop off my trunk with the men tossing bags in the back of the truck. In usual military style, they have asked us to show up eight hours before our flight is scheduled to leave. A group of USO volunteers is serving coffee, juice, and sweet cakes inside the base at the rear of a large auditorium. There are several short briefings, but none that share any new information. I look around at the troops who are saying goodbye to their families. Departing husbands kissing wives and departing wives kissing husbands. Many have brought children. Perhaps it would have been better to drag Meredith and the kids along, but in my mind I was deployed the moment I walked out the front door, not to return until I had served my time. Being trapped in this limbo of kiss and cry just seems like salting the wound.

We board an ambulance bus with a red cross painted on the side and travel across a golf course from Lackland Air Force Base to Kelly Field. In the distance, F-16 fighter jets and C-5 cargo planes stand ready on the flight line. Inside the bus, I recognize many faces from the hospital, but I know few of their names. It's strange to think these people are going to be my surrogate family for the next four months.

The bus arrives at the Kelly Field terminal, where a DC-10 jet plane marked WORLD AIRWAYS is fueling up on the tarmac. The flight attendants assure us they have safely carried a lot of troops to the Middle East recently. Somehow that doesn't cheer me, but I appreciate the effort. I ask for my usual Bloody Mary mix but settle for tomato juice.

When we land in Baltimore the flight attendants let us off the plane to stretch our legs. I am suddenly reminded how much colder Baltimore is than Texas. Fifteen years ago when I was still in medical school at Johns Hopkins it wasn't so bad, but tonight on the tarmac the wind churns off the Atlantic and cuts through my fatigues.

We take on more passengers, many of them reservists from hometowns across the eastern United States. It is probably tougher for them going through their preparations alone;

they're not part of a large hospital group like I am, and I can't imagine too many of them expected to go to Iraq when they first signed on.

We cross the Atlantic in the dark of night. Soon after the sun has risen through the cloud cover at 25,000 feet, we descend and land in Shannon, Ireland. It is my first visit to Ireland, but I won't see much more than the airport. We find a pub on the second floor of the terminal, and I order a thick, rich pint of Guinness stout. I try to savor it—thanks to General Order 1-A Section 2-c this is the last chance I'll get to drink alcohol for several months.

I hardly have time to finish my drink. The announcement comes across the loudspeakers and we're on the plane again to Qatar. I drift off to sleep; wake twenty minutes later to watch American movies as the snow-covered peaks of the Alps pass beneath us. Eventually the pilot announces our descent into Al Udeid Air Base. From the window, I see dirty brown sand stretching in all directions. The sky, an overcast tan-gray, blends into the land and disguises the horizon. We land softly and taxi to a cluster of tents and aluminum buildings. Our flight attendants bid us good luck, we thank them for their kindness, and climb down the steps to the runway.

The landscape is drab brown, the cold air thick with the smell of wet sand and jet fuel. Ahead of me, the line of troops slinks forward like a well-camouflaged snake, soldiers in their DCUs (desert camouflage uniform) nearly indistinguishable against the background of mud and gravel. We mill about under rain shelters, tired from the trip and unsure of what comes next. Our group of 120 troops makes up about one-third of the replacement medical staff for the combat support hospital in Iraq. From fresh-faced nineteen-year-old airmen, to a fifty-year-plus grizzled reservist who has left behind his private practice to again serve his country, we are doctors, nurses and medical techs from scattered origins across the United States.

On first glance, Qatar is not an attractive country. Named with the Arabic infinitive "to exude tar," it is a desolate, flat, one-hundred-mile-long peninsula that juts from the eastern edge of Saudi Arabia into the Persian Gulf and at no point rises to more than three hundred feet above sea level. But for what it lacks in physical beauty it makes up for in wealth. The country is incredibly rich—with billions of barrels of oil reserves accounting for one of the highest gross domestic products in the world.

We pass through customs and hop a bus from the flight line of Ops-Town to the residential area of Al Udeid Air Base. Approximately two thousand troops are stationed here, and thousands more pass through every day as they enter and exit the Area of Responsibility. With a small group of surgeons, I wander through the maze of tents and trailers. We find the telephone and Internet facility and I take a moment to let my wife Meredith and my three boys know I have made it this far safely. She sounds wonderful, though she can't believe I have been traveling for so long and still haven't made it to Iraq. She wishes me well and I wish her my love.

At the Post Exchange (PX), I thumb through a phrasebook and practice the Arabic, *"Ana duktur,"* for "I am a doctor," and *"Ayna al-alam?"* for "Where is the pain?" Through the years, I have picked up medical phrases in a few different languages but Arabic is not one of them. I still remember *"Sou doutor"* in Portuguese and *"Mwen dokte"* in Kreyol, from humanitarian missions to Brazil and Haiti. During my residency, I worked with a plastic surgeon who told me all a surgeon needs to know in another language is the phrase "Hurry up!" He could recite it in twenty different languages and would shout it repeatedly until the nurses brought him the instrument he needed. I just hope I can expand my repertoire to include a few words of courtesy.

The flight to Iraq is long and loud. Conversation is impossible over the roar of the engines. We smile at each other and stare at the naked, utilitarian guts of the cramped C-130 cargo plane. Some drift off to sleep. Packed so closely in the heat and held upright by body armor and Kevlar, I sweat through my uniform T-shirt and boxer shorts. Toward the end of the flight, a garbled message broadcasts over the loudspeakers that we are about to land in Balad. The pilot asks us to strap in because he is going to make a combat landing. I do as told, bracing in my seat, and tightening the nylon straps across my shoulder blades. Suddenly the pilot banks the plane sharply right, then left, then drops it like a stone, the cabin pitching to a steep slant as we dive towards the runway. I reach between my legs and grip the aluminum frame of my jump seat to try to stay tucked in the fetal position. It is no use. Each time the plane shifts directions I am thrown violently against my neighbors, our helmets smacking together, and our bodies tossed about like dolls. It is nauseating, but at last it ends. The wheels hit the runway with a thud and we coast to a stop. As the tailgate lowers with a mechanical whine, the temperature in the plane drops noticeably and clay-scented air rushes into the hold.

We gather our packs, secure the Velcro closures of our armor, fasten our chinstraps, and tramp down the ramp of the plane and onto the runway. It is a cool, clear night in Iraq. Stars glitter in the sky, their light filtering through a haze of silica dust suspended in the air. Powerful flood lamps splash light across the runway, which runs far into the distance. The phosphorescence brightens a nearby cluster of tan buildings squatting in the dark mud. As the C-130's propellers sputter and halt, I begin to hear the competing growls of different vehicles crossing the flight line.

In an Alaska Shelter surrounded by cement barriers we are in-processed to Balad Air Base. Halfway through a session of briefings obscured with acronyms my exhausted mind can barely decipher, I step outside to use the Porta Potty next door. Hardly have I begun, when the closeness and privacy of the dank space is invaded by the sound of a siren. I finish and zip up. On my way back to the shelter, a sergeant yells to me, "Hey! We're in alarm red! Take cover!" He looks at me as if I am crazy to be walking around so nonchalantly. I stop in my tracks and pivot my head around, searching for the danger that has him so distressed.

"Huh?" I grunt.

He hurries over, waving his arms anxiously, and practically drags me to a nearby concrete bunker, a long low structure roughly six feet high, six feet wide, and one hundred feet long. Its roof and sides are formed by a shell of concrete meant to protect against fragments from mortars and rockets. I enter to find the rest of my mates hunkered down along its walls. Orthopedic surgeon Tom welcomes me with a chuckle and says, "We thought we lost you already, Chris."

I am far too tired from the trip to feel much sense of urgency, even if there is real danger out there. From the looks on my colleagues' faces, I can tell I'm not the only one who is exhausted. "How long do you think we'll be here?" I ask. Tom opens his eyes for a moment and shrugs. Down the length of the tunnel-shaped bunker, I can see about forty troops cramped together in the darkness. Up and down the line, flashlights blink on and off as people peer around in the dark confines of the concrete. I root for a package of half-crushed cheesy crackers in one of my cargo pockets and take advantage of the moment to have a little snack. An airman across from me accepts my offer of one of the less-crushed cracker sandwiches. With our bulky body armor and Kevlar, it is hard to even shift our weight without jostling the adjacent troop. Someone cracks in the darkness, "Hurry up and wait!" Even though we are in a war zone, no one seems particularly scared—sleeplessness seems to dull fear. After fifteen minutes, the "all-clear" sounds over the base's Giant Voice System and we return to the Alaska Shelter.

I meet up with the other surgeons and we commandeer a white Ford van to carry our equipment to the trailers across the street from the hospital. The roads of the base are paved, but the asphalt is hidden under a dark, thick mud. As we travel from the flight line, Humvees and deuce-and-a-half trucks cross the base roadways on mysterious errands. The compound surrounding our trailers is covered with a stew of sludge: stagnant rainwater, and smooth, rounded river stones the size of potatoes. Already dead tired, I get out of the van and drag my heavy trunk across the quadrant to the trailer I've been assigned by the Army housing office. The hooches are divided into three sections, each with its own door and short triad of steps. A five-foot wall of olive green sandbags rises midway up the height of the trailer.

I knock on the door of hooch A4 and am greeted by two sleepy faces—troops who tell me there is no room, and they are living there for another four months. The second trailer I am assigned houses a female nurse. General Order 1-A forbids co-ed housing, so I'm back to the Army housing office for a third attempt. I swing open the door of hooch A9 to see flimsy wood paneled walls, an upright locker, and a cot. I stumble in, leaving a sizable mound of mud and pebbles at my threshold. There is an overhead light and several 220V electrical outlets. The place looks like an empty container at a self-storage facility.

My hooch-mate isn't here, but his bunk and gear are neatly arranged to the left side. Everything is well organized, though a thin coat of sparkly dust coats the floor and every horizontal surface. I drop my gear to the floor and unfold an aluminum frame, green canvas cot on my side of the room; unroll my sleeping bag and toss my pillow to the head of the bed. I want nothing more than to go to sleep, but there is still one small task to take care of before I drop off for the night. I unload my electric hair trimmer and step outside in boxers and a T-shirt.

There is no one around; the housing compound is silent. The oscillating razor feels warm against my forehead as I slide the stainless steel blade across my crown. I suppose shaving my head is a kind of acceptance of the rotten situation of having to be here. I feel a lot of things—loneliness, fear, concern for my family back in Texas. As the last vestiges of my stateside life pile in black-gray clumps on the wet earth, I take a full breath. No longer is there any doubt that my part in this war is real. Until now, the war has been something I have critiqued from afar, a missed opportunity to deal with the stability of Iraq as a world community. But now I am in the middle of this mess, and it is very personal.

# First Night on Call

THE WEATHER SURPRISES ME. I've seen many pictures of soldiers sweating under layers of armor in Iraq's 130-degree heat, but they don't reconcile with the nippy, overcast landscape that greets me each morning when I step outside my hooch. Last night I used the combined heater/air-conditioning unit to take the chill out of the air. It makes a terrible racket and manages to spit dust even in these muddy conditions. At least it provides some uniform white noise to drown out the staccato clatter of Black Hawk helicopters and the roar of F-16s, traversing the sky, day and night.

This was Saddam Hussein's premier air force base and flight school until we took it over at the start of Operation Iraqi Freedom in March of 2003. It has the longest and best runway in the country, but little else remains of the Ba'athist regime. The buildings are imported, prefab trailers and warehouses made of aluminum and ticky-tacky. They all look just the same. There are a few low, flat cinderblock structures that predate the war, but for the most part the facilities are hastily constructed buildings, made from stamped metal and pushed-together trailers. A twelve-foot-high chain link fence topped by rolls of razor wire surrounds the base.

The first few days are a bustle of paperwork and other arrangements designed to get our team checked in and ready to

Murals in the Balad Air Base administrative offices celebrate Iraqi air power. This artwork remains from the pre-invasion period when the facility was Al Bakr Air Base, home to two squadrons of Iraqi operated MiG-23 fighter jets.

work. We visit the base clinic for shots and rummage through the armory and supply depot for weapons and armor. As we shuttle through a variety of buildings I start to get a feeling for the topography of the base—laid out in a near square, three-by-four miles along the edges. Its dimensions hug two enormously long runways that allow a steady stream of flights in and out of the facility.

Forty miles north of Baghdad, close to the geographic center of Iraq, the base serves as the hub for the majority of military activities. Housing for the twenty-thousand soldiers and five-thousand airmen stationed here stretches in well-ordered rows, like the grounds of a never-ending trailer park. In our scurry to complete administrative duties, we pass by many of the creature comforts the base has to offer: several gymnasiums, a movie theater, the Base Exchange (BX) department store, barbers, rows of shops in an Iraqi bazaar; even familiar restaurants like Burger King and Pizza Hut.

My daily ritual begins in the Cadillac, a white trailer equipped with sinks, urinals, toilet stalls and showers. A long row of benches runs down the center, and the floor is covered with thick, perforated rubber mats similar to the ones in front of the dishwasher station at the seafood restaurant where I worked as a kid. On the walls are signs that read, COMBAT SHOWERS IN EFFECT. Combat Showers are ninety seconds long. Take thirty seconds to get wet, and turn the water off. Lather up and then take sixty seconds to rinse. There is no joy in a ninety-second shower, but today, like every morning, I clean the essential parts and head out for the hospital.

The sun is rising over the Tigris River, and far-off palm trees line its bank. Outside the wire, the local farmers work the land. They tend sheep, goats, and cows; some till the fields with tractors. Men and women work together. Everywhere the ground explodes with growth in green rows. The growing season in this part of world begins in early January, well before the scorching summer months. Life seems to go on as if war were something far away and of little concern to the people of Balad. Children go about the business of being children. They wear brightly colored clothes; one rides a donkey, slapping his rump with a twig, turning him in endless circles. Two others chant in raised voices and laugh at the end of each verse.

Just a short walk away, on our side of the fence, the hospital is a honeycomb of twenty-five tents and hollowed-out trailers. Organized as branches off two parallel corridors, the layout runs north and south. One side includes the emergency room, radiology, pharmacy, laboratory, operating rooms, and the surgeon's area. The surgeon's area is at the crossroads of the hospital, and is called the PLX because it is at the junction of the pharmacy, laboratory, and X-ray room. The other corridor forms the spine for a series of tents that sprout off like ribs, and contains the intensive care unit, wards, clinic, dining hall (DFAC), morale, welfare & recreation facility (MWR), command area, and morgue. The interior of the tents is lined with vinyl fabric to defend against dust and chemical attack, and muddy water runs in rivulets under the tent flaps.

Our crew of twelve surgeons is replacing a team that has been running the hospital for the past four months. Both teams are a mixed bunch of general surgeons and specialists. There are orthopedic surgeons, neurosurgeons, an ophthal-mologist, an otorhinolaryngologist, a urologist, and a maxil-lofacial surgeon. Most of us are from Wilford Hall Medical Center in San Antonio, but others are from smaller Air Force hospitals or reservists who have been called up for duty. We gather around last night's surgeon on duty (SOD), transplant specialist Gary, who succinctly lists the operations he per-formed.

"We had two BKAs and one neck exploration for gunshot wound. Tikrit sent us a Marine with appendicitis, and there was one guy in the medevac from Baghdad who needed a sec-ond washout of abdomen after taking shrapnel to the liver from an IED two days ago. We got him on the 0400 flight to Germany." His calm tone suggests this is a usual night's business. He goes on, "Today we have two more washouts of abdomen to do on the Iraqi policemen, and I think ortho has a few limb washouts too."

"How'd the appendectomy go?" asks Trevor, the fresh SOD taking over for the day.

"Went well, but it was perfed so I'm going to keep him around a day or so before deciding if he needs to be evacuated. He's a mechanic back in Tikrit so we might be able to get him back to duty within two weeks."

The hand-off from one doctor to the next is seamless and orderly. Compared with the veterans, our new team isn't as well integrated; some of us are meeting for the first time. We are mostly silent, trying to absorb as much information as possible so we will be ready to run this hospital.

I know Bill. He is a trauma surgeon back in San Antonio, and combat support work is right up his alley. We started together as new surgical staff at Wilford Hall two years ago. It was comforting to begin the job with another newcomer, and Bill and I became fast friends. Here he looks even more gung ho than he does at home: his usually close-cropped, black hair is shaved to a bald shine; he wears small professor's spectacles framed in black wire rims; nods his square jaw emphatically as surgeons Gary and Trevor discuss the successes of the night before. If it weren't for the modern markings on his uniform, his shaved head and classic features could easily be the picture of a nineteen forties doughboy standing in a drab military tent somewhere in France.

But Bill and I won't be working together tonight and my call partner General surgeon Trevor, is far less familiar. He works at Wilford Hall, but I haven't seen him since he left for Balad four months ago.

"So it's you and me tonight!" he says cheerfully. I can tell the outgoing crew is happy to see the arrival of replacements.

"I don't know how much use I will be on the first night," I tell him. "So teach me whatever you can."

"Don't worry; the hospital really makes it easy for the surgeons. We do so many cases that the whole system is set up to get the patients in and out of the OR fast. We've all gotten into a rhythm of doing things the same way every day. You'll pick it up fast."

I look at him and nod. My surgical training has prepared me for emergency situations, but combat support surgery is completely new.

For a while, the business of the hospital carries on as shifts of nurses tend to patients recovering on the wards. Trevor and I hang out in the PLX where he teaches me how to use the computer system and maintain the spreadsheet of current patients. Off-duty surgeons go to dinner and bring us back cheeseburgers and french fries in Styrofoam take-out boxes.

Sometime after dark, I hear the approach of a helicopter—its rotor beating the air with a chopping sound that grows steadily louder, until I can't hear the person next to me. The ceiling and walls of the PLX tent flap, and tendrils of dust curl around the damp edges of the floor. Seconds after it passes my beeper goes off, summoning me to the ER for a trauma call.

I move quickly. Nurses and technicians ready a station with equipment and medication for the patient's arrival. The ER nurse is one of the twenty or so Australian personnel who staff our hospital. She calls out, "Get the RT." A tech sprints off and quickly returns with the respiratory technician, who wheels in an oxygen tank, tubing, and mask. The twenty-by-eighty-foot tent is an orderly beehive of activity. It is easy to distinguish the seasoned veterans from the new arrivals; nearly every staff member is trailed by a replacement troop furiously trying to absorb information.

Two ER techs wearing protective eyewear and sound-dampening headsets roll the patient in on a NATO gurney. They are trailed by a medic clad in a flight suit, body armor, aircrew helmet, and night vision goggles. The techs wheel the patient into the trauma bay and flip out legs from the gurney to support the head and feet of the litter. I move in and look down at the patient lying on the stretcher. It is a child who looks to be about two years old. I had expected to see a soldier or at least an adult, and the sight of a child is jarring. I can't tell yet if this chubby-faced child is a boy or a girl. The medic tells us he is a boy who was shot in the head about forty-five minutes prior and needed to be intubated in the field. He has been stable in the helicopter, but hasn't moved his limbs or opened his eyes. I ask the medic if he knows how this baby was shot, but he only answers, "Crossfire at a checkpoint." Streaks of dried blood trail down the boy's hair over his bruised right eye. There are small petechiae (broken blood vessels) across his forehead and the bridge of his nose. His face is so swollen it is hard for me to open his eyes, and below them, a clear plastic endotracheal tube leads into his throat; the shoebox-sized transport ventilator puffing breaths into his lungs at regular intervals.

Though new, I am the surgeon in charge so I direct treatment and run the trauma. We check his vital signs, and I start an IV catheter to augment the emergency intraosseous line the medics have inserted into his shinbone.

I nod approvingly as the RT reports, "Tube's in good position; good bilateral breath sounds."

The nurse calls out, "Heart rate 140, pressure 80 over 48."

"Give 400 of saline," I tell her.

The tech cuts away the baby's clothes and I check his torso, inspecting each limb for any other sign of injury. We roll him on one side to examine his back, securely supporting his head and neck, and then lay him to rest on the stretcher.

"Get me one of those heated blankets to cover him, and I want 10 of mannitol. Let's get the CT scan as fast as possible." We bundle him up snug. After a quick chest X-ray, we wheel him to radiology for the CT scan of his brain. I pile another warm blanket on the little boy because the CONEX container that houses the scanner is cooled to fifty degrees to keep the circuits from overheating. We step behind the leaded shield that will protect us from the radiation and I put a page in for neurosurgeon Larry to return to the hospital.

He arrives at the scanner a few minutes later wearing his

physical training uniform with the matching reflective Air Force jogging suit. His head is shaved bald, which seems to be the trend around here. Back in Texas he wears his light blond hair spiked up in the front. I've known him for several years at Wilford Hall. He is a wonderful surgeon, a specialist for children who has been able to help some kids with life threatening brain tumors. At home our paths don't cross too often because his work has him operating inside the skull, and mine has me operating everywhere else on children. The operations we've done together have been mostly ventriculo-peritoneal shunts, where Larry implants a tube into the spaces of the brain, and I tunnel the other end into the abdomen so fluid can run off, relieving pressure inside the skull. When he sees me in the control booth of the scanner, he smiles and clasps my arm.

"Hey, Chris, good to see you. How're you liking Balad?"

"This is my first call night; I'll let you know in the morning."

"What's the story on the child?"

"A two-year-old boy, shot in the head. Hasn't moved since he got here, but he was intubated in the field. His pupils are normal. We just got him in the scanner."

Larry swivels around quickly and sits at the terminal behind the leaded shield. He works the controls with prescient hands. Cross-sectional images of the boy's brain, like slices of a bread loaf, scatter across the computer screen. The bullet has lodged in the parietal lobe of his right brain. It is surrounded by a thick halo of blood, and a gritty trail of bone fragments marks the path of the projectile. The swollen right hemisphere is squeezing the left as each vies for space within the confines of the skull.

Larry has seen enough. "He needs a craniotomy. Let's get him to the OR now and get some blood ready." We rush the boy to the operating room. The scrub tech lays out instru-

ments on a table draped in a sterile blue sheet. The anesthetist, Sally, prepares medications and gas canisters on the
anesthetic cart, her short sand-colored hair bobbing back and
forth as she works. The circulating nurse positions the boy on
the operating room table, with his head propped on a small
padded support like the donut at the head of a massage table.
She shaves his curly hair with an electric trimmer, revealing
a small puckered crater in the skin of his scalp, high above
his right eye, where the bullet entered. The nurse scrubs his
bald head with a deep orange-brown Betadine soap solution.

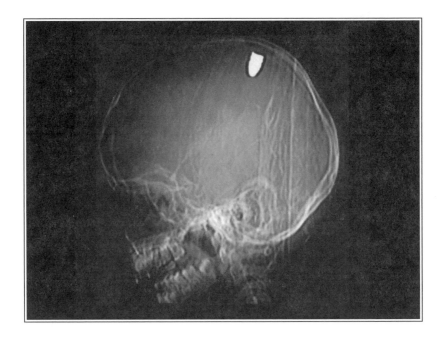

I follow Larry to the surgeon's scrub sink. "Can I scrub
in and help you?" I ask. It has been ten years since residency
when I last opened a skull, but I know I can provide an extra
set of steady hands. And when a boy has a bullet in his brain,
there is not much time to consider whether or not you've been
properly vetted.

Larry is immediately gracious, thanking me and saying, "At Wilford Hall I usually have a resident in on a case like this, but here we are the residents and medical students."

We drape the boy's head in sterile blue towels, until only a patch of orange scalp is visible. Under the sheets, his chest rises and falls gently at the automatic rhythm regulated by the anesthesiologist's cart. Larry cuts a long curved incision in a wide arc above the boy's right ear. We work with forceps and the Bovie electric cautery pencil, peeling back layers of skin, fat, and muscle to expose the surface of the skull. The bullet's entry site looks like a neat round hole cut for ice fishing. Larry drills three holes in the bone and uses the edge of the drill to connect them into a triangle. He teaches how to turn the flap of bone by gently peeling it off of the hard dura mater membrane that protects the brain.

Under the dura, the boy's outermost brain mass bulges through the drilled hole. The space around it is surrounded by bloody fluid, a dark purple bubble underneath the membrane. Larry cuts open the dura and exposes the damaged tissue. He works methodically in concentric circles, using the bipolar Bovie to cauterize the bleeding edge of intact brain. He directs me to use suction and absorbent cotton sponge to clear his view of the injury. I give him plenty of room. Like an attentive medical student, I anticipate his moves but don't get in the way.

"Careful not to suck up any normal brain."

"Got it." I guard the tip of my suction catheter as I guide it across the soft pink edges. Brain surgery is not my field of expertise, but after years of operating on the tiniest babies, precise surgical control is. Larry trusts my steadiness and expertise, and our hands work in a synchronized ballet of burn, debride, blot, suck, until we can stem the oozing.

After extracting the bullet, Larry removes dead tissue,

fragments and debris. We wait several minutes to ensure that the bleeding has stopped for good, and that the swelling is under control. Larry calls for materials he needs to close the wound, and the circulating nurse passes them to the scrub tech. We carefully secure the flap of bone with small brass screws and plates. Then we place a tubular rubber drain to remove any new bleeding, and sew shut the layers of his scalp.

Larry smiles, "The bleeding could have been a lot worse. Praised be to Jesus we got him through that."

Larry and I haven't ever talked about religion, but here in the middle of war, his words don't seem out of place. He clasps my hand in appreciation and pats my back.

"I can tell you that we don't keep too many of these open gunshot wounds to the head alive back in the States."

It does feel like a milestone to be past the gauntlet of my first operation in Iraq, even if I was only the assistant. The boy is moved off the operating table and rolled to one of the three ICU tents, where nurses will monitor him through the night. I take advantage of the lull in activity to grab a Gatorade from the DFAC. It is tough to tell it isn't lunchtime. The hospital's business runs around the clock, and the night shift is just as hectic as the day shift. Sixty or so techs and nurses stand in line, extending their cafeteria trays forward as the line workers scoop mounds of steaming noodles and beef stroganoff onto their plates. After sweating away in the heated OR, it feels good to replenish and hydrate.

But the spell doesn't last. I am promptly summoned to the ER again, where I meet up with Trevor. Our patient is a young man who has been shot in the abdomen. He stares up at us with wild eyes and moans in pain. His face is pale. He gasps for air from an oxygen mask. A twenty-two-year-old Iraqi policeman, he has been shot on his right side, just where his ribcage joins the abdomen. The bullet has left a hole the size of a silver dollar, and eviscerated a loop of his small intestine. It protrudes from his abdomen like a swollen bloody bagel. The intestine still looks alive, but one end of it has been shredded by the projectile and leaks green fluid. It is clear he is headed for an operation. We make sure he is getting air into his lungs, place large IVs into his veins, and scoot him into the OR.

As Trevor and I scrub in, the anesthesiologists move quickly to stabilize the man. They get him intubated and anesthetized, pour fluids into his veins. As soon as the emergency release O-negative blood is available, they squeeze it into him. The circulating nurse has shaved and prepped him from chin to groin by the time we get into the room to don our gown and gloves. It has been a long time since I have taken care of adult trauma victims. Fortunately, it is very rare for the young victims of trauma I treat back home to need an operation. But now I stand above a six-foot-tall man weighing as much as I do. Trevor has been doing this nearly every night for the past four months. I follow his lead.

With a long incision, we open his abdomen from his sternum to his pubic bone. The gap lets us quickly view all the abdominal organs and stop the bleeding. It is the standard trauma laparotomy. After warning the anesthesiologist of the danger of sudden blood loss, we slit open the thin peritoneal membrane containing his internal organs. Out rushes a flow of dark blood mixed with rice and intestinal fluid. Working in concert, we stuff large absorbent sponges into each of the four corners of his abdomen, and another four into his pelvis. One by one we unpack the sectors of his abdomen, suctioning up blood and bits of undigested food as we go. When we remove the sponges under his liver, dark blood wells up in a torrent. I quickly replace the old sponges and hold pressure against his spine with my fist.

"I think it's the vena cava," I tell Trevor. We peek again, and sure enough the bullet has blown a hole in the body's largest vein. The bullet has come to rest somewhere behind the cava in the thoracic spine and I can feel prickly shards of shattered bone. The duodenum and right kidney seem pretty torn up too. I count the layers of organs that have been injured: liver, colon, small intestine, pancreas, duodenum, vena cava, spine. I run a quick mental tally and realize I am treating the five worst gunshot injuries I've seen in my life.

"His pressure's dropping," the anesthesiologist warns.

Trevor and I stand on either side of the open patient, our hands working in unison. We both lean forward, our heads nearly touching from across the table, to get the best view into the deepest recesses of the man's abdomen. Each time Trevor peels back a layer of tissue, I slide my hand over his to retract the tissue from his line of sight. Whenever blood spurts from yet another torn blood vessel, I blot away the liquid and apply pressure. Trevor pauses to look up at me from across the OR table. "He's losing a lot, we'd better call for a whole blood drive."

# Blood Drive

WE HAVE A LIMITED SUPPLY of blood in the hospital. Just one patient with substantial loss can deplete our reserves. If a patient needs numerous transfusions, they become deficient in factors such as platelets, not found in stored blood. For these reasons, we use fresh whole blood transfusion. Whole blood isn't stored in the blood bank; it is stored in the "walking blood bank." Even though it is two in the morning, soon after the request goes out over the Giant Voice System, there are two-dozen troops lined up in the hallway outside the blood bank.

Back in the OR, Trevor and I work to repair the tattered vena cava. As I carefully expose it, Trevor applies a broad, curved vascular clamp to hold the two sides shut and control the bleeding. I run a seam of blue Prolene suture along the torn edge and we remove the clamp. Blood is leaking from a few small points, but some strategically placed stitches do the trick.

The first unit of donated blood arrives and there is more to follow. We find the locations where the bullet has punctured the intestines, staple them shut, and remove the portions riddled beyond repair. For the large piece of intestine hanging out of the man's side, I tie off mesentery blood vessels and snip off the damaged segment. Altogether we remove four spans of intestine, eighteen inches in length.

The incredible energy carried in the rifle round has pulverized a portion of his body wall. I cut away shredded muscle and shattered rib fragments until I reach healthy firm tissue. The hole in his side now measures six inches across. Through it I can see his bruised liver. We continue with the transfusions, but his blood pressure stays dangerously low. The major bleeding has stopped and it is time to get him out of the room before the operation kills him. The bullet responsible for this damage will stay where it is, lodged in his spine. We stuff his belly full of sponges to hold pressure against the injured organs. A suction tube leeches blood and fluid from his swollen viscera. I wrap him in dry blankets, shifting his bony frame carefully on the operating table, and he is rolled off to the ICU.

I honestly have no idea if he will survive. I am drenched in sweat, my scrub top stuck to my chest. My pants are covered in blood. Bits of gore cling to the toes of my boots.

Trevor walks out of the ICU, calmly. "Want some coffee?" he calls out over his shoulder. "The DFAC will have a fresh batch. It tastes horrible, but it'll be hot."

His scrubs are soaked with sweat and blood, but he is not too concerned. He yawns then hums as he starts down the corridor.

"Was that a typical case?" I ask him. I quicken my pace to catch up to him. "I think I've only seen three caval injuries in my whole career."

"Pretty much; every part of the body can get hit by bullets or shrapnel. No matter what it is, we've probably seen it injured here."

"So this is normal?"

"Normal? I don't know if I would use the word normal."

After a bitter cup of DFAC coffee with a slurry of grounds at the bottom, I change into fresh scrubs and wander over to the MWR tent to see if I can e-mail home. On the way I visit the ICU to see how the two-year-old boy is doing. His vital signs are stable and he is starting to move his extremities. With Larry's care, I am confident he will survive. I walk down the corridor and turn into the MWR tent. There are shelves of donated toiletries and comfort items, racks of magazines and paperbacks heavy on the spy and romance genres. A few troops are using the computers, and one is asleep on the couch. The computers are wired to the Internet by satellite.

I sit down at one of the laptops and check my e-mail. As I hoped, Meredith wrote and included messages from our three boys. Our youngest boy, Reid, is just shy of his second birthday. He doesn't have much to say. Griffin misses me and wants to know what I've done with their toys. Each of my sons picked out a toy for me to take to Iraq. Ben gave me the autographed baseball my father used to teach him to play catch, Reid sent a fluffy yellow duck that quacks "Jingle Bells," and Griffin chose a Shrek doll that makes a farting noise when squeezed. I have barely unpacked my gear, but the baseball, duck, and Shrek are waiting for me on top of the trunk back in my hooch.

I tell Griffin not to worry about the toys or me. I tell all the boys that I have a very important job for them. They have to take good care of their mother while I am gone. I need them to be big boys and behave so it is easy for her.

Nothing I could tell them would offer any semblance of normalcy to this absurd state of affairs. I just hope they are handling it better than I am. When I think of the boy with the fresh incision on his head, it is easy to be thankful for my healthy family. I click "send" and make my way back to the ICU to prepare for morning rounds.

# A Night at the Movies

ON SUNDAY, RESERVIST SURGEON DONNY from Hawaii invites some friends, including me, to join him at the movie theater to celebrate his birthday. Still wearing our PTUs, we head over to the Sustainer movie theater, and relax at a round table in the lobby, drinking near-beers from the concession stand as we wait for the movie to start. Donny and I are in good company with nurse commander Diana, trauma nurse Rose, and ER nurse Patty. Everyone looks happier and more relaxed than they do in the hospital. I have the Bitburg near-beer, which is not as good as the Beck's near-beer. I hear the St. Paulie Girl near-beer is tasty, but none of them can hold a candle to beer-beer.

After some lighthearted jokes about Donny's age, we filter into the theater for the movie. The Sustainer is a large auditorium left over from Saddam's reign. The screen is fifty feet tall, and the theater has a large lower level and upper balcony. The seats are upholstered in red velvet with bare patches where countless asses have rubbed the pile off the fabric. I can imagine Saddam sitting front and center in the balcony as pilot graduations take place on stage. Now the balcony is a retreat for soldiers seeking a dark, private location during the movie.

We get good movies: first-run showings that screen just weeks after they premiere in the US. Uncle Sam spares no expense to help us forget we can't be with our families.

Right before the lights go out, we watch a short film from the Army Signal Corps. Images of soldiers serving in wars past and present flash across the screen while "The Star-Spangled Banner" erupts from the speakers. Our assembly snaps to attention and stands in respect as the first bars of music play. Scenes from Normandy, Iwo Jima, Vietnam, Kuwait, fill the screen. Here in this air-conditioned theater, I can't help but think that I have it easier than most of them. I wonder what role I will have as a serviceman in my country's defense, though I have no ready answers.

The movie tonight is *Closer*. It is a meandering, cerebral examination of people in relationships, longing for the one they cannot have. It has an audience somewhere, but it is not the best choice for a bunch of hepped-up nineteen-year-olds with M-16s. The pained, awkward dialogue scenes and drawn out promise of physical satisfaction are not what our company needs tonight. To make matters worse, the audio track keeps dropping out and the projectionist falls asleep, missing the reel changes. The audience begins to rebel with catcalls and improvised lines. Soldiers wave their rifles at the screen and trace Natalie Portman's breasts and crotch with circling red target lasers.

I join an exodus of many other troops and leave the movie early. My new mode of transportation is a battered mountain bike inherited from the hospital's outgoing dietician. The chain is coated in a patina of rust, and the vinyl seat is patched with duct tape, but it gets me where I need to go. I ride out of the theater compound and onto the darkened streets of the base. Nondescript figures wearing camouflage and toting weapons trudge drearily along the sidewalks. At street corners, I pause to ensure I am not flattened by a speeding Humvee. My ultra-bright reflective belt is strapped around my waist, but visibility is poor through the cramped windows of a dusty Humvee. I roll by rows and rows of darkened hooches behind stacked sandbags. After passing the Cadillac, I round the curve into H4 housing and slide to a stop at the door to my hooch. Snuggled into my bunk, I examine my bare walls, listening to the Rolling Stones.

Ten minutes later, I find myself in the ER awaiting the arrival of another casualty. The Black Hawk crew sounds frantic on the radio. They are coming in fast with a troop blown up in an IED attack. They don't have vital signs. CPR is in progress. It is an ominous report. There is no joking as we ready the trauma bay. I glance around to see that all teams are ready. The ER crew is standing by with IV equipment and monitors. The radiologist stands at the back of the tent with her technician, who is preparing the portable X-ray machine. The pharmacist has wheeled in a cart with drawers of emergency medications and is preparing syringes with saline flush. The laboratory technician, waiting to receive blood specimens, tends an Igloo cooler with emergency-release blood. Donny stands ready, as well. We will operate together if this patient goes to the OR.

Near the storage rack I see Tom, the orthopedic surgeon who fixed the dodgeball player's leg. It happened last night after we sent teams from our hospital to compete in the base-wide MWR dodgeball tournament. As the players rushed for center court, one of the big and tall Army soldiers jumped for a ball and collided with another player. His shinbone buckled and folded with a resounding crack and he hit the ground and held his leg up, the lower half hanging at an abnormal angle from mid-calf. Blood welled from the spot where the broken bone had pierced through the skin. Before the poor guy could utter a word, he had five surgeons pouncing on him and splinting his leg with cardboard boxes and athletic tape. Luckily one of the other teams in the tournament was an ambulance crew. They backed their bus up to the gym entrance and pulled out a stretcher. The young soldier was transported to our hospital, where Tom took care of his leg. He was to be evacuated to Germany to have a metal rod placed across the fracture. It was a bad thought, but I couldn't stop it from entering my mind. "Lucky dog, he just got handed his ticket home."

I ask Tom about the soldier.

"Already on the way to Landstuhl. We finished right before the airevac collected patients. He should get an intramedullary rod placed by tomorrow."

I exit the ER and cross the walkway to the helipad. I like ushering patients into the hospital because it helps me pick up details from accompanying medics. There is a moment of stillness in the post-midnight air before I hear a Black Hawk approach from the south. The beat of the rotors quickly grows to a roar, and a wave of dust crests over the barricade. The dim green glow of night vision goggles on the pilot's face is the only visual trace of the swiftly descending aircraft. It drops fast and lands hard on the cement helipad, bouncing roughly on its wheels.

Two ER techs with a NATO litter meet the medics, who are flinging open the cargo door. Together they slide the stretcher deftly from the helicopter onto the litter stand and roll toward the hospital at a half-run. One of the medics rhythmically pushes his gloved hand down on the patient's chest, continuing CPR as they cross the helipad. I join them at the walkway to the ER. The medic is panting hard from his efforts. His ballistic visor is flipped up, and I can see sweat streaking the grime on his face and neck. His whole upper body dips with his effort to continue compressing his patient's chest. He shouts his urgent report to me. "National Guard truck driver, 'bout twenty-years-old. Took an IED blast on Route Golden. Near traumatic amputation of both legs. Tourniquets on both legs and left arm, facial burns. No vitals at scene or in transport."

These few details have told me it is all bad. The patient took enough of the direct blast of the explosion to tear both legs off. If there wasn't an immediate cardiac arrest, the rapid hemorrhage probably brought one on fast. We will still go through the basics of trauma resuscitation: the A, B, and C of airway, breathing, and circulation.

The soldier is encased in a thick vinyl body bag. At the head of the stretcher, his puffy charred face juts out of the opening of a silver survival blanket. A clear plastic endotracheal tube has been threaded between swollen lips, and one of the ER techs is puffing breaths of oxygen into this tube with a bag-valve assembly. We wheel the stretcher into the ER and park it in the bay closest to the OR. The respiratory tech transfers over to house oxygen and continues ventilation. The ER tech assumes compressions to relieve the medic. Nurse Rose unzips the body bag, starts cutting off the soldier's uniform, and hunts for fresh veins to draw blood and insert IV catheters.

She gasps aloud, "It's a woman!"

I look down from where I am checking for a pulse in the patient's neck. Our patient is indeed a young woman. Dirt and charred fragments of her uniform cling to her breasts. Ugly mottled bruises discolor the skin over her sternum where CPR has cracked her breastplate.

I suddenly cannot make any sense of the scene. Black nylon tourniquet straps bite deeply into the flesh of her thighs. Her legs below the knees are reduced to shredded meat. I feel no pulse in her carotid artery, and above the neck, her head is a swollen, burned, androgynous mess. I feel the wind sucked out of me, and a pressure in my chest. "A woman," is all I echo back hoarsely.

We continue our resuscitation. A sequence of trauma life support steps gives her every chance to recover her vital signs. But none of the medications or maneuvers stirs her heart to beat again. She has bled out and died. None of our attempts to save her made any difference. She died in spite of the medics' heroic effort to get her to us so quickly. I call the code, solemnly thank the crew for their hard work, and note the time of death.

I look around the tent at a mixture of shocked, horrified faces. I've treated many women who have suffered non-combat trauma before. Some made it, some did not. But I cannot wrap my mind around the cold reality of a woman soldier being killed in battle. Her death seems so wrong. I struggle just to stand on two feet in front of her bedside.

Donny puts his hand on my back and tells me, "You ran a good resuscitation, Chris; this was a tough one. I don't think anything we did could have saved her."

"It doesn't make any fucking sense. She can't be more than twenty."

"She was a soldier. She did her duty as well as she could tonight. Just like you did."

"It doesn't matter what I did, she's dead."

"You gave her your best. Her family will appreciate that, and she would have too," he consoles me.

One of the young techs is hard hit and softly sobs in a corner of the tent. Patty and Diana hold her and comfort her quietly. I pace aimlessly around the ER, picking bloodstained shreds of uniform and medical equipment from the ground and tossing them in the big red biohazard bags. Why it's different for a woman to die in war, I can't say. I only know it feels different.

# Election

THE ENTIRE BASE is on edge because today will be the first free Iraqi elections since Saddam Hussein was removed from power. Only hours from now the Iraqi people will elect a National Assembly tasked with forming a new constitution. The Election Commission has prepared six thousand polling stations around the country, which is roughly the size of California, in anticipation of this historic event. US troops will guard the polls as the Iraqi National Guard does not have the organization to handle such a widespread job. I worry for the troops who are going to be spread thin at too many polling stations. Last Wednesday, in a harbinger of violence, a number of police officers and members of the Awakening Council—an ad-hoc armed militia of Sunni fighters—were killed in an ambush southwest of Diyala.

Even inside the wire it has been tense. Now we wear identification on base and must present it to gain access to buildings. We avoid the perimeter where we would be easy targets. I carry my weapon, a 9mm military-issue Beretta M9, at all times. A few days ago a rocket landed just a few feet from the entrance of the ER. Fortunately, it was a dud, or not properly armed. If it had detonated, it would have taken out most of the ER and one of the clinic tents.

Most of the Iraqi shells are forty years old and don't work, but that knowledge doesn't help me sleep. Every helicopter passing overhead wakes me. When I hear the impact from a mortar or rocket I try to judge how far away it is. I listen for additional booms, expecting the enemy to adjust their aim and send subsequent rounds closer to target. As I walk around the base, I keep an eye out for the nearest bunker. I have figured out the points between my hooch and the hospital where it is better to run forward, or make an about face and flee, if there is an alarm red. Each time I speak with Meredith, I make sure our closing words are ones I would be happy with as the last thing she hears from me.

Worst of all are nights when I have no duties. I collapse onto my mattress, dusty and achy from long operations and the sweaty trip back to the hooch, but unable to sleep. Lying alone at night, I wonder what will happen to my children if some stray mortar takes me out.

We worry the election will multiply the number of patients coming our way. Under the direction of our commander, Rocky, we've prepared for election day by stockpiling extra blood and running mass casualty drills with empty stretchers. Coalition loyalists like Awakening Council members and Iraqi policemen are not the only targets. Already the insurgency has vowed to attack polling sites and wash the streets with voters' blood; in fact, the Sunni community has threatened to boycott the whole thing. Civilians are fair game in this war.

Yesterday, when Rocky had us all gathered in the recreation tent, he gave an earnest speech, no notes, slides, or microphone. I found myself hanging on his every word. He called on us to consider the eagle, a symbol emblazoned on our crest. He likened the head of the eagle to God, guiding our purpose; the wings of the eagle to freedom and democracy; the talons to courage and sacrifice. He told us he had seen courage in our ranks and warned us that during the election we might be called upon to treat seriously injured soldiers. "When injured troops come your way, they will not seek your sympathy," he said. "They will seek your help. It is your duty to help them without fear or hesitation."

Rocky is a tall man, at least six-foot-two. His hint of jowls and receding hairline betray his age, and he always has a pair of reading glasses perched on the bridge of his nose. In addition to running the hospital, he is a plastic surgeon and pitches in to help when there is a patient with a particularly difficult wound to repair. In another world he would be the perfect image of the mature, benevolent doctor who could put any patient's nerves at ease.

Except for the far-off noise of a helicopter crossing the base, there was no sound in the tent but his voice. We stood at ease, still and attentive, without any of the slouching and distraction that usually accompanies a commander's call. When it was over, we filtered out of the tent.

"I've never heard a speech like that," I said to Bill, as we walked back to the hospital across the muddy gravel.

"Yeah, I felt like I was with Henry V on St. Crispin's Eve."

"Do you think he's right? Do you think something bad is going to happen?"

"Not to us."

Polls around the country open at 0700. For the first two hours we see a trickling in of Iraqi civilian casualties from the many mortars, suicide bombings, and IEDs directed at the polling stations. Normally, the backup surgeon would leave the hospital to exercise or wander the PX, but Bill sticks around, just in case. We alternate between watching CNN and taking care of the arriving casualties. In his weekly radio address, President Bush states, "As democracy takes hold in Iraq, America's mission there will continue." Interim

Iraqi President Ghazi Al-Yawar is one of the first to vote, and pretty soon reports come in of an excellent voter turnout. Photographs from polling sites everywhere show broadly smiling Iraqi men and women, proudly displaying fingers stained purple from the ink used to mark who has voted.

Mid-morning a bomb goes off in western Baghdad. Twenty minutes later, a Black Hawk lands, bringing us an injured seven-year-old boy. He is bundled in blankets, and bloody bandages cover his head and face. Bill and I listen as the boy's father relays the story. His words are translated by Kasim, one of the interpreters who report to the ER. Kasim is a young Iraqi man, twenty-four years old, always neatly groomed and modestly dressed in Western clothing. He has the uncanny ability to translate a patient's words into flawless English.

The injured boy's father speaks to Kasim in urgent bursts of Arabic. The man is a farmer and postponed his work for the day because he wanted to be one of the first people in the country to cast his ballot. His son accompanied him to the polling station. As they waited in a long line for their turn, an explosion one hundred feet away rocked the ground and shattered windows. The people in line were knocked over. The father recovered and searched around for his son. He found the boy lying unconscious with blood streaming from his face. A fragment of shrapnel had struck his son's forehead, tearing the skin and knocking him out.

I already know that children do not fare well in modern warfare. Their proportionally larger heads, coupled with the fact they are closer to the ground, make children a particularly vulnerable target for a fragmentation weapon like a buried IED. That knowledge may not help me heal the child, but at least I am prepared.

I look him over from top to bottom and place a bandage over the laceration on his forehead. He flails about and mutters incomprehensible sounds. My team in the ER wheels him to the CT scanner. Bill and I review the images of his head with our radiologist. The boy's skull is fractured, but we also get the good news that there is no shrapnel or bleeding in his brain. The neurosurgeons take a quick peek at the CT results, but they have another patient to care for, a middle-aged man with multiple fragments of metal embedded deep in his brain and surrounded by bleeding. Bill and I will have to take care of this boy on our own.

He has been intubated by anesthetist Sally and lies perfectly still and peaceful as we prod the fringe of skin on his forehead. For several minutes we work in silence. We shave hair surrounding his complicated scalp laceration and remove the larger chunks of char and dirt. The nurse scrubs his wound clean and we trim away dead skin and tissue. The wound goes down to the bone, and I can feel the broken edges scrape against each other like loose tiles as I work the skull. Fractures through the durable skull indicate a forceful explosion, but thankfully the bony vault has served its purpose of protecting the brain from a more devastating injury. The boy is in no risk of dying. We irrigate the flesh until it is clean, close his scalp layer after layer, and stitch his torn skin back together. He gets through the operation well. Hopefully he will recover with faculties intact.

We peel back the sterile blue paper drapes covering the boy's face and body. He sleeps peacefully in an anesthetic-induced slumber, breathing calmly to the rhythm of the ventilator. Something about the Cupid's bow arches of his upper lip and the rounded chubbiness of his pink cheeks makes him look like my four-year-old son, Griffin. I look at Bill through the clear plastic splash guard of my mask.

"My son isn't even one yet, and I see him in all the kids we treat," he says. It's as if he read my mind.

"How is your son?" I ask.

"Okay. He had a cold for a few days, but it's out of his system." As we lift the boy from the operating table to the rolling stretcher, Bill asks me honestly, "Do you think these elections are going to matter enough to make it worth what this boy is going through?"

"I don't know, but I've got to hand it to these Iraqis for turning out. I'm feeling pretty embarrassed for the time in college I skipped voting because the parking lot was too full."

Patients continue to arrive. There is a seventeen-year-old girl, shot in the neck outside the polling place. She was standing with her family when gunmen sprayed the crowd with bullets. Our vascular surgeon, Brent, operates to explore her neck for injuries to the carotid or jugular. She survives the operation, but the sad truth is we cannot treat the damage to her spinal cord. From the looks of the CT scan, she may never walk again.

An elderly woman comes in with multiple fragment injuries from an IED detonated near the lines of people waiting to vote. Dirty fringes of torn skin hang from the edges of her wounds. Old rags are wrapped around her shins to stem the bleeding, and her bare feet are callused and cracked. Lying on a green canvas stretcher, she shows no sign of pain, proudly holding up her right index finger, stained purple with ink. She is a living statue of national pride and bravery, and the spirit that drove her to the voting booth gives me hope for the future of Iraq. After her X-rays, Donny and Tom bring her to a third operating room to clean her legs and stabilize her broken bones.

It hurts to see children and old ladies shot up and blown apart. They do not deserve to be victims of war. Back home, politicians triumphantly proclaim the arrival of democracy in Iraq. President Bush, in a TV message from the White House, describes the election as "a resounding success" and praises the Iraqi people who "have refused to be intimidated by thugs and assassins." But they don't see the mangled bodies coming into the ER.

There is good being done here today. The Iraqi people are stepping up to the plate and voting. They are voting for a better future for themselves and their children. For decades Iraqis suffered under the reign of Saddam Hussein, a sadistic monster who institutionalized rape, torture, and murder to tighten his stranglehold on the country. When Kurds in northern Iraq rose in defiance, he killed them indiscriminately with poison gas: man, woman, and child. But today the injured entering our doorway raise their ink-stained fingers in a gesture of victory.

Beyond the hollow threats of weapons of mass destruction and links to Al Qaeda, seeing this great thing happen makes even a cynical critic of war like me hopeful. Even if this war was fought for the wrong reasons and young American troops have suffered for it, I will be the first to embrace a positive result. As I watch the reports of suicide bombers and attacks on voters in Baghdad and Mosul, I am praying and wishing for their safety. The danger the Iraqis are facing as they exercise a right that we take for granted points out how fortunate we are to live free. Who am I to say the pursuit of a better life isn't worth the cost?

# Hostile Fire Pay

THOSE OF YOU not in the military may not know, but our corporation, the US military, tries to quantify the personal risks and demands of war in financial terms. You may have heard of hazard pay in movies, but it isn't just a Hollywood device. The other day I wove through the concrete bunkers to visit the base finance office and start my Family Separation Allowance. No sum replaces the absence of a loved one, but the intention is appreciated. There are a number of other benefits.

- Hostile Fire Pay/Imminent Danger Pay is given for any month you spend in a designated Imminent Danger area: $225 per month.

- The Combat Zone Tax Exclusion relieves you from paying income tax on wages you collect in the area of responsibility.

- Hardship Duty Pay gives another $50-$150 per month depending upon how primitive the camp.

- The Savings Deposit Program allows you to collect 10 percent interest on the portion of your pay you elect to deposit during your deployment.

While deployed, you can also request a travel voucher accrual for each month. Anyone who travels for their corporation is familiar with this concept: the per diem. With the travel voucher accrual, you can claim your per diem each month as you earn it, rather than one lump sum at the end. Personally, I don't want someone else making interest on my money.

The bitterest sum is the $250 Family Separation Allowance you draw each month for being away from your family and/or dependents.

I am immensely grateful that Congress has acknowledged that the sacrifice of separating from my family to serve my country is worthy of notice. The amounts are nice, but it is the recognition that I appreciate. That brings up another point. I work for you. You have paid your taxes. They have gone into our national coffers, and 67 percent of the $1.1 trillion-dollar budget goes to national security and defense. A fraction of that money makes its way into my pocket and supports my family. Thank you for your work. I say this on my own behalf, and for the 1.5 percent of the US population who chose to serve in the Armed Forces. But I can't stay here forever. I need to get back to my core.

# Patriot Detail

BALAD IS NOT just the disembarkation point from Iraq for the living; it is also the port of exit for the dead. When a fallen troop departs from our airstrip, we honor their sacrifice in a ceremony called Patriot Detail. It happens almost daily. All troops on base are welcome to attend and many do. I attend tonight's ceremony because I was on duty at the hospital the night these men died.

It was a wet and dreary Sunday evening when we received a distraught platoon leader suffering from hypothermia. He commanded Task Force Danger's Blue Platoon, which was on combat patrol in a column of four vehicles. It started out like many missions they had run. They were out patrolling their area of responsibility, scouting for insurgents along one of Balad's canals that run swift this time of year. It was raining hard, the path was dark, and they used minimal headlights to conceal the fleet from their enemy. It happened in seconds; the second Humvee in formation tipped off the slick edge of the canal and overturned into the rushing water.

Three young men were riding in the truck, all in their early twenties. They came from Florida, Louisiana, and Iowa. The platoon leader immediately sensed that he had lost contact with the vehicle. He halted the remaining three vehicles and rushed to their aid. They put out a call for help, which was quickly answered from our base. Firefighters and helicopter pararescue jumpers (PJs) arrived on the scene and plunged into the cold water. One firefighter, twenty-nine-year old USAF Staff Sergeant Ray Rangel, was swept away to his death attempting to save the men. The other rescuers risked their lives as well, suffering hypothermia as they extracted the soldiers from the submerged vehicle. Unfortunately, the three men had been trapped under water for far too long and drowned.

We treated the platoon leader for minor physical injuries. He had suffered nothing more than a few lacerations and scrapes. We wrapped him in layers of blankets stored at one hundred degrees. Our first aid was of little consolation to him. He screamed out in anger and cursed; he coughed and snarled, "They were my responsibility!" We all felt horrible. He was too furious at himself to hear what we were saying. What he couldn't recognize then was that his quick action saved the other men in his platoon.

Soon we received five other rescue personnel from the scene. They were all drenched to the bone and dangerously chilled. As we worked to warm them and bandage their wounds, one PJ frantically explained, "That road was a death trap. Parts of the embankment had crumbled into the canal. It zigzagged across the plain so you could never tell how far the canal was from the road. If Sergeant hadn't brought the convoy to an immediate halt, we probably would have lost two more of the vehicles in the water."

Lying there wrapped in blankets, shivering like a newborn, there wasn't an expression left on the platoon leader's face. All I could think to do for him was call for the chaplain. Sometimes when there is nothing useful that medicine or a doctor can deliver a chaplain can be of greater assistance. When he arrived he held the platoon leader's face tightly between his hands and spoke to him quietly from inches away. "You cannot hold onto this. You must forgive yourself. These horrible things happen and good men are taken from us in war, and there is no way we can understand why. We are soldiers, we must carry on, it is the only way we can honor them. You are a good man, and this hurts because you are a good man. Their families will be grateful they were led by someone who cared for them." He then whispered, "Turn to God." The platoon leader pressed his tear-streaked face against the chaplain's chest. I haven't seen him since that moment and I hope that his heart finds peace.

I report to the terminal at 2300 and queue up with other troops, about sixty in all. There are combat troops and office clerks ranging from airmen to colonel. I do not recognize other personnel from the hospital, but the faces are just like those I work beside every day. Fresh young kids barely out of their teens and veterans with more than twenty years service under their belts; firemen skirting the fence line—all of them come to bid farewell to a fallen colleague. After minutes of silence, a chief master sergeant walks out of the terminal. His DCUs are crisp and clean, every crease pressed to a razor's edge. His shaved head shines as if he has waxed it, his brown skin reflecting the flood lamps along the edge of the runway. In a rich baritone commander's voice he begins, "Thank you for coming out tonight to pay respect to our fallen brothers. They made the ultimate sacrifice in defense of our great nation, and we will give them a fitting farewell." At his command, we line up in two files and "taller tap." The troop ahead of me is inches shorter, and I tap his shoulder and step forward in line. When all is done, we are two columns of thirty troops, neatly arranged from tallest to shortest. As we wait, two F-16 fighter jets take off, afterburners shrieking at terrific volume, as orange and blue cones of flame stretch out from behind their engines.

A C-130 cargo plane approaches our position, turns 180 degrees, and lowers its loading ramp at its tail. Fluorescent tubes in the cargo bay cast a semicircle of soft light onto the runway.

We march out in silence, flanking the two columns of firefighters to our right, and take position toward the back of the plane. In front of us, soldiers in full battle rattle line up in formation. All counted, there is a cordon of over 150 troops standing at attention behind the plane. Ambulances from mortuary affairs pull onto the runway. One by one, the human remains containers are carried past our ranks by a detail of six soldiers. The containers, shiny steel and aluminum boxes, are draped in the rich red, white, and blue folds of an American flag.

We salute each of the honored dead at a three-second tempo. I am cold. It is thirty-two degrees, and the wind at my back is chilling my bare scalp and making me shiver. I think of the families of these four brave young men and try to hold the most respectful salute I can muster, one worthy of their service and sacrifice.

The loadmasters busy themselves securely fastening the men to the floor of the cargo bay. With gloved-hands, they cinch the straps tight, ratcheting the clicking wheels of come-alongs. Finally our dead brothers are tucked in for their journey. The ramp is raised, sealing off the cargo hold and hiding the occupants from our sight. The engines kick over with a whine and a roar. The C-130 rolls away, slowly at first, but gathering speed. As the pilot throttles up, the plane lumbers past the flight line and lifts into the air, the groan of the turboprops gradually receding from our senses. Once the plane has disappeared into the darkness, the chief releases us from formation. Wordlessly we stamp our feet to keep warm, and shuffle off to our respective duties.

Days go by, and the casualties keep coming. It seems that every day at 1700 we are sure to get the victim of an ambush or IED detonation. Friday, my wingman and SOD for the night, thoracic surgeon Zack, calls me in at 1830 to join him. As I enter the PLX, trauma nurse Rose shakes her head ominously, "He's a sick one." The story is familiar. In nearby Balad city, our soldiers detected three insurgents arming an IED. When the troops engaged them, the insurgents panicked and prematurely detonated the explosive. One insurgent perished immediately in the blast. Another took major blast injuries to his chest, belly, arms, and legs. Just as quickly as they had neutralized the insurgents, the American soldiers gave them emergency first-aid and called in a dust-off. We received the seriously injured man and Zack rushed him to the operating room.

The patient is a mess. His entire body looks like it was run through a meat grinder. There isn't a square inch of skin on his body that is not burned, bleeding, or sprouting metal shards. An endotracheal tube feeds into his mouth and multiple IV catheters protrude from his limbs and groin. The techs have cut through the folds of his beige robe. He carries no other possessions, and his footgear, if he had had any, was blown off in the explosion. Like many of the Sunni insurgents we have treated, he is tall, well fed, even tending toward obese. He is a would-be murderer, blown up by tools intended to kill our soldiers. Yet in this nearly lifeless state, pathetic and losing quarts of blood, it is hard to imagine him as any type of threat. I look for signs in his swollen face of malice, but all I see is a dying man who needs our treatment.

We call for the orthopedic team to help stabilize his fractured limbs. In a matter of minutes, there are four surgeons
and two physicians' assistants frantically working to save his
life. But the blood loss is massive. I put out a call over the
Giant Voice System and shortly thereafter a dozen volunteers
have lined up to donate blood to save the life of this insurgent.
The blood comes, but too late to make any difference. Despite
their generosity, he has bled out; he may have survived each of
his injuries alone, but together they are too much. His death
leaves me cold. As a team we feel like a failure whenever we
lose a patient who arrives at our hospital alive. We gave this
enemy the same care we give our troops, we did everything in
our power to keep him breathing. But he was on a mission to
kill my countrymen and may have succeeded if he were still
alive. How am I supposed to comprehend his death when my
duty as a doctor to heal contradicts my duty as an officer to
defend?

    After days of intense activity, we are fortunate to have a
period of calm. We tend to our recovering patients and take
them through the maintenance operations of washing wounds
and placing feeding tubes. The Iraqi policeman shot on my
first call night has been a frequent visitor to the operating
room. I have cleaned his abdominal cavity many times, but it
seems that every time I am successful in repairing one leak
from his intestines, another crops up. Luckily, he has the
strength of his youth, and so far he is hanging in there.

    I touch wood and hope this lull continues. There is a palpa-
ble feeling of the staff collectively exhaling and stealing some
extra rest. We surgeons mill about the place and collect in the
PLX to thumb magazines, medical textbooks, and check our
e-mail. The OR nurses bring back letters and boxes from mail
call. I open a care package from Meredith and share some

Swedish Fish with Donny. He trades me a delicious can of Maui onion macadamia nuts sent to him by a friend. We catch Bill sleeping on one of the ratty, imitation-leather couches in the PLX. He is an easy target for a candid photograph, and I snap a few shots, waking him momentarily with the flash. He growls like a disturbed dog, baring his teeth before drifting off to sleep again. Such is the price for falling asleep in public. Donny chuckles and shakes his head. I should just let Bill alone, but the photos will be just the right touch for morning report.

Later that afternoon, I raise my eyes to the sunshine for the first time in days. I decide I need a little break on the bike to try to clean out my head. Up on wheels, with a steady breeze passing, I feel worlds better than I did in the hospital. I bike past our housing compound and head out to the track. The fat tires splash through muddy puddles on the cracked pavement. My vest weighs heavy on my shoulders, and it takes a measure of concentration to keep the thirty-five pounds of body armor I wear centered over the bike. It feels good to work the cramps out of my legs and have the broad blue sky over my head, rather than the olive-drab low ceilings of the hospital tents. I scan the road for the many wide Humvees that mo-

*(left panel)* The M998 High Mobility Multipurpose Wheeled Vehicle (HMMWV or "Humvee") was the primary vehicle deployed in support of Operation Iraqi Freedom. The vehicle lacked sufficient armor to protect occupants from IEDs. In 2004, the Army contracted O'Gara-Hess & Eisenhardt Armoring Company to produce the M114 "up-armored" Humvee *(right panel)* and armor kits for existing vehicles. Mine Resistant Ambush Protected (MRAP) vehicles with V-shaped hulls have replaced Humvees as the safest ground transport.

tor around the base, and pause at intersections to allow their hulking forms to pass.

My thoughts return to the public uproar made about Humvee armor before I deployed. The early ones had cloth or thin metal doors. They were vulnerable to IEDs in cities or on convoy. An explosion under the vehicle could injure the soldiers' legs and groin through the floor. Earlier in the war, Humvee drivers scavenged junkyards for steel, using plasma cutters to fashion thick metal panels and mount their own defenses. Newer Humvee shipments are up-armored at the factory. They have full underbody armor and tiny layered-glass windows, as if visibility wasn't already challenging enough. What kind of Humvees did the Blue Dragons have? That I do not know. I do know that no amount of armor could have saved the drowning men.

# Meal, Ready-to-Eat

MRE STANDS FOR "Meal, Ready-to-Eat," and after a full day of operations I sure was ready to eat. MREs can be shipped, trucked, dropped from a plane, left in the hot, cold or wet, and are a soldier's primary foodstuff when he is out of garrison. I don't know the shelf life, but it's long. The last time I had eaten an MRE was during my Health Professions Office Indoctrination Course, or as I like to call it, fake boot camp. Since then, there have been all sorts of space-age improvements to the MRE, most significantly the heater pack.

Last night I scurried away to our new call room, which is the above ground bunker that formerly belonged to the Iraqi Air Force under Saddam Hussein. We surgeons commandeered the structure and keep it stocked with every creature comfort we can lay our hands on. With a pager on my belt and a two-way radio at my side, I was ready for a dinner adventure. I started by breaking open the package and spreading out the contents. I had chosen Menu # 9: Beef Stew because I thought stew left a wide margin of error in preparation and safety. I'm saving grilled beef patties and chicken enchiladas for after I have survived the basics.

The appetizer was something familiar, crackers and grape jelly. The crackers were a bit dry and brittle, but the jelly was a sweet and wholesome reminder of all things American. After making quick work of the *amuse-bouche*, I proceeded to the main course. The food comes in a foil-lined pouch within a slim cardboard sleeve. The MRE heater is a mystery to me. You simply open the plastic bag, pour water on the filter packet of ominous-looking black crystals, and presto, you've got a hot meal. There is a lengthy warning label on the heater. If the military told me, "Don't worry, just shut up and roll up your sleeve!" about the anthrax vaccine, but required a paragraph to warn me about the heater, it surely deserved my full attention.

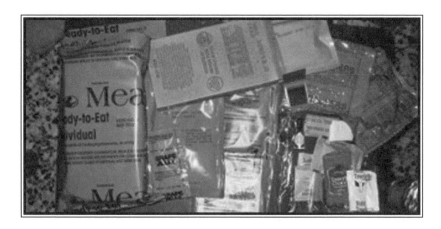

Unfortunately, I began before reading all the instructions. I got as far as STEP ONE: ADD WATER TO DOUBLE LINE ON BAG. I say unfortunately because, soon after pouring in the water, the heater became too hot to hold, and I had to hastily cram it into the box with the pouch of beef stew without reading the rest. Actually, I'm proud I read even the first step of the instructions. That's further than I usually get before trying something on my own. I did gather that my MRE would give me energy for top performance. I also learned that I need three meals each day in the field, and that the MRE provides thirteen hundred calories. I was advised to eat the high carbohydrate items first, such as crackers.

While the stew was warming, I mixed my chocolate dairy-shake in its own pouch with six ounces of water and scarfed it down. I slid the heater out of the piping hot cardboard sleeve, and read enough of the directions to realize I folded it wrong. I corrected the situation by folding it properly and tilting the box up on two paperbacks. While waiting for the stew to finish in my tiny kitchen, I opened what I thought was a napkin and found squares of tissue. Either my military benefactors wanted me to refrain from wiping my nose on my sleeve, or they were predicting, rather correctly, that I would be in need of tissue squares after eating my MRE.

The warmed pouch felt comforting to the touch. As instructed, I kneaded it to distribute the temperature evenly, but felt like I was crushing my potatoes. I tore open the packet greedily and sampled the nourishing contents. Like everything served here, it required the zest and camouflage of hot sauce, so I was happy to find a miniature bottle of Tabasco sauce packed in the bottom of the MRE box. I quickly licked the pouch clean and moved on to dessert. Cookies with pan coated chocolate discs sounded suspicious. I'm surprised it wasn't an acronym, like "cookies with PACHODS." There is no need to be cryptic: PACHODS are Government Issue M&M's. The cookies were not what I would call "good." A better description would be "rock-hard with a vague aftertaste of soap." The Chiclets gum wasn't much better. Still, the meal had its intended effect. With a full belly, I soon collapsed fast asleep on the couch.

# The Body Politic

TONIGHT THE GATE GUARD calls during rounds. "I've got an Iraqi couple here with their two kids, and they are requesting admittance to the hospital. They've got a four-year-old boy with scald burns on his leg. They've also got an eighteen-month-old son they want you to look at, but I can't figure out what they think is wrong with him."

He tells me the family first visited the hospital in downtown Balad. The Iraqi doctors there said, "Go see the Americans."

"Send them in."

When they reach the hospital the father is ebullient, shaking everyone's hand. He is portly but vigorous, with shiny skin and eyes. "Hello, my American friend!" he exclaims in English, repeating this again and again to everyone he meets. His face is all smiles, with a rich black moustache and a middle-aged man's receding hairline. Open at the collar, an off-white *dishdasha* covers him from shoulders to ankles. "Thank you for helping the peoples of Iraq!" he cries. The boys' mother, herself much younger, is pregnant and carries a bulging round bump of a belly on her slender frame.

Their four-year-old boy is a worried little man, with a tiny burn on his thigh from an accident in the family kitchen. He spilled a mug of hot coffee onto himself, an injury all too common at our hospital. He stares at me with terrified eyes as I kneel to his level and very deliberately uncover his wound. A small and shallow burn, it will heal quickly even if ignored. I sit with the parents while Zack gently cleans and dresses the wound. The boy gives a loud shout but calms down quickly once his leg is wrapped in a cool, medicated dressing.

We hand the child back to his mother. "Thank you," she tells us quietly, smiling with gentle assurance, and nodding at her husband's expressions of gratitude.

Their eighteen-month-old boy is a completely different matter. He is none too happy to meet me and glares at me with suspicion and anger. I sit close to give him a chance to get used to me, but his brow furrows in disgust and streams of tears run from his eyes. He tightly grips a Beanie Baby frog given to him by the ER tech and uses it to wipe the snot from his nose. Somewhere back home a child in some church group can be satisfied that their donation is going to good use. The boy's eyes dart between his father, his mother, and me. He turns his little body away from me defensively and leans into his mother.

Kasim joins us in the little clinic tent next to the ER. The boy's father speaks to him in hurried Arabic and keeps pointing to the child's diaper. Kasim translates, "The problem is in the boy's diaper. He has always been this way and he is different from the other son."

The father hushes the child as he undresses his son. He lays the boy on his back on a NATO gurney and says, "My son is growing well and is strong; it is only his penis that is different."

I examine the child and immediately understand. His genitals are neither those of a boy nor a girl. He has a condition known as intersex anomaly, in which a person's body forms some male parts and some female parts. He appears well otherwise—healthy skin, strong bones, normal vital signs. As I inspect his flat empty scrotum and small nubbin of a rudimentary penis, I try to formulate some way I can explain this to the parents. Already I can tell I have a difficult discussion on my hands.

Kasim keeps looking curiously over my shoulder. The boy's parents are watching me too. When they ask Kasim what is going on, he clucks his tongue brusquely, urging them to be patient.

I put the boy's diaper back on and place the child in his mother's arms. Then I sit down to face the parents and consciously allow an expression of calm to spread across my face. "I see what you mean that his penis is different. I have done everything I can with my hands and my eyes; I need some X-rays to learn more about his internal organs that my hands can't reach."

The external exam is one piece of the puzzle, the internal organs are another. Unfortunately, our hospital doesn't have the capability to give me the most definitive piece of information: a chromosomal analysis of the child's gender. I will have to make the best with what I've got.

Kasim translates this and the parents nod and smile. "Thank you!" the father says, then *"aywa, aywa,"* an Iraqi colloquialism for "yes." These parents, like many others, are eager for X-rays, CT scans, MRIs, and other Western technology. It is one thing to have a person touch and gaze upon their child, but the objective eye of a machine is never wrong. "We knew the American hospital would be better," the father confides to Kasim. "The Iraqi doctors wouldn't even help us."

As we prep the child for tests, I send the rest of the family to the DFAC to catch a late dinner. The child is so worked up it takes a mild sedative to complete the radiographic studies. After he calms, I obtain the X-rays without hindrance. It is now midnight, and the rest of the family rejoins us. They will spend the night with us in the security of the base. I study the X-rays and sit down with the family to share what I have learned.

Kasim speaks on my behalf. "I am happy to tell you that your child seems to be very strong and is growing well." The father and mother seem pleased; they turn to look at each other, then turn back to me and nod. "What I have to tell you next is difficult to explain, but I will do my best and take as much time as we need." I have picked up a little Arabic, perhaps enough to order a coffee in a restaurant, but I know my ability with the language is wholly inadequate for what I have to say next. Even in English, the diagnosis would be difficult to communicate without upsetting the family.

"The X-rays show me that inside your child's belly there is a womb and ovaries. Even though he looks just like a boy on the outside, his internal organs are those of a girl."

Kasim is an excellent interpreter. Together we have explained to mothers and wives that their loved ones need emergency surgery, or have been fatally wounded. In all of this, he has been straightforward and mature and never faltered in his duty. But tonight when I tell him the child is internally a girl he gasps and pauses to compose himself before delivering the message in Arabic. The mother pulls her son closer to her chest, and the father stares at me with wide, disbelieving eyes, stepping backward to shelter his family. I explain further, reviewing the details of the tests step by step.

"Your child is a female pseudohermaphrodite. His genetic material is the code for a female, but an imbalance in the function of his hormones has caused the growth of genitals that look like a rudimentary penis. He has not formed a normal vaginal orifice or labia, but internally he has a uterus and two ovaries. When he reaches puberty those ovaries will slowly start to change his body into that of a young woman. Our hospital does not have the specialized genetic and hormonal laboratory tests for me to determine exactly what defect has caused his intersex anomaly, but the characteristics of his anatomy are unmistakable."

The parents just stare. I try to maintain a steady, open expression on my face. What must they think—an American doctor telling them their wide-eyed little boy is internally a girl with a womb? I keep my voice supportive as I continue, "It is important for us to remember that he is healthy and strong, and he is not in any danger."

The mother begins to cry, her dark round eyes welling up with tears.

"I know you have raised your child as a boy, but the female hormones inside him are very powerful. When he is about nine-years-old, his body will start to form breasts and hips. Eventually he may even have monthly menses." Gesticulating with his hands, Kasim speaks to the parents soothingly in Arabic. They hold each other closely and look worriedly at their child. The mother has not stopped cradling her son close to her bosom.

If I had met the child when he was born, I would have advised his parents to raise him as a female; adjustment and growth would be easier. But in Iraq, where access to health care is a problem and the male child is prized, the decision requires different considerations. I tell them, "I know it will be difficult to make a change, but I expect that your child will have an easier life if raised as a girl."

"*La!*" the father explodes forcefully. "*La! La!*"

Kasim jumps back. The father imposes himself between his family and me, lifting his chin defiantly and glowering down at me. I am less surprised than Kasim at his outburst, but I'll admit I'm not sure how violent he will become. Looking at his eyes, frozen in their sockets, I realize nothing I can say to him will change his mind. I try to assure him, "This boy is your child. Nothing happens to him unless it is your decision. I only want you to know as much as possible about his condition so you can take good care of him." I tell him there is no emergency and no decisions have to be made now. I am in a difficult position and unsure if I have done the best for this child. All of my instincts and usual medical advice for intersex anomaly are predicated on the cultural specifics of the West.

"Even with this diagnosis, he can live a full and happy life. If you choose for him to continue life as a male, he will need treatment when puberty approaches. He will require hormone therapy to develop male characteristics. If his ovaries are not removed, he will start to develop female features."

The father returns to his wife's side, sits down on the bench opposite me. He looks at his wife hopefully, but his hope is naïve. Gender isn't just a snap of the fingers. Given the state of the country's medical resources, I don't even know if hormone therapy will exist in Iraq by the time the boy needs it. "It is completely up to you if you choose to tell any family or friends this private part of his life," I tell them. The man inhales deeply and comforts his wife. Once I have convinced him the child will be able to live a healthy life as a boy, his hostility relaxes and he smiles broadly at Kasim and me. I don't know if I have done the right thing by giving him the promise of his son back. But I have managed to assuage his anger.

From his mother's arms, the child looks up at his father with a mixture of love and trust. The father is soon up and making rounds, thanking everyone in the hospital he can lay his hands on. I learn a new idiom from him. He says when he brought his children to the Iraqi hospital they turned him away like an "Ali Baba." Iraqis don't have a high opinion of Ali Baba of the forty thieves fame. Iraqis call insurgents, traitors, and thieves Ali Babas to disparage them. But this wasn't always the case; stories change here, myths evolve. In pre-war Baghdad, Saddam erected a monument glorifying the moment Ali Baba and his servant Morgiana vanquish the thieves lying hidden in oil jars, waiting to ambush him. There is perhaps a morality tale hidden somewhere in the tale of the forty thieves killed in boiling oil, but morality is rarely as simple in Iraq as it is in fables.

The family of four departs the next morning in search of an endocrinologist at Medical City in Baghdad. I send them off with copies of all the boy's X-rays and a detailed letter describing what I have found. Soon after they leave, I call Dr. Yusuf in Baghdad. Dr. Yusuf is an Iraqi doctor from Balad, a medical jack-of-all-trades, and our liaison at the local hospital. I first met him on one of many weekly rounds with us, evaluating the progress of our Iraqi patients. He is a valued friend who helps us find homes for Iraqi patients not strong enough to return to duty or live independently. I don't understand why he has stayed on at his post at the hospital when so many others have left, fearing for their lives, but we are thankful for him. Dr. Yusuf answers his satellite phone, calm and polite as always.

"Dr. Yusuf, this is Chris at the Air Force Theater Hospital. I want to ask you a question about a patient. I am sending a female pseudohermaphrodite to Medical City in Baghdad to find an endocrinologist. Will they find much help there?"

In his usual manner, optimistic but noncommittal, he answers, "Perhaps they will. There was a very good endocrinology department at the university there before the war, and if there is anywhere in Iraq they will find help, it is there. It is such an interesting case. Thank you for helping yet another

Iraqi family, Dr. Coppola. But perhaps there is little the family can do."

"In the US this family would be counseled to raise the child as a female, but when I told the father this he refused to accept it."

"That was to be expected, given the status of women in our society. Don't worry about that child; his family will take care of him. There is far worse that could befall a child in Iraq these days. I will make some calls—I'm sure at least one of the endocrinology professors has stayed in Iraq."

At least one, he says, but who knows what will happen given the state of chaos in Baghdad. I can only hope that this family will make the trip safely.

# Skin

OFFICIALLY, I AM ON DUTY every five days or so as the SOD. It really is not very demanding unless we have a mass casualty (MASCAL) event. Unofficially, I am always on call for injured children who are brought to the base. Since I am the only pediatric surgeon in the area, I wouldn't want it any other way. One night at midnight I wake up to my pager beeping in the darkness. I pull on my uniform and boots and trudge out to the nearest phone near the Porta Potty. "Hey Chris, thanks for calling back," Larry says. "The ER called you because a couple of burned kids came in. Bill's working on them right now.

"There's an American troop with shrapnel in his brain on the way up from Baghdad. I'm just answering the phones because I'm hanging out until he gets here. I've got to see if he needs an operation before he gets evacuated to Germany."

"Tell Bill I'm on my way in."

I grab my helmet from the hooch and bike into the hospital. The base is silent except for the far-off rumble of trucks at the KBR depot. I assume the children have been transported in by surface ambulance since I haven't heard the sound of a Black Hawk. There is no way I could have missed it; their flight pattern runs right over my hooch, and I sleep so lightly and fitfully that the slightest noise wakes me. My guess is that these burns occurred in some sort of domestic accident. So many homes are without power, and dozens of children are getting burned on open flames. Every other day we hear the story of a bonfire erupting from generator fuel mistakenly spilled on the dirt floor of a kitchen.

In the ER tent, Larry is sitting at the triage desk, uploading pictures of a sunset over Balad. He writes a daily newsletter to the members of his church back home. Somehow he manages to get them a quick message before the busy daily life at the hospital begins. He catches me looking at the screen.

"It's the least I can do for them—I know they're praying for me every week. Your patients are back there."

"Cooking fire?"

"No, insurgents. Bill's going to be glad to see you; they're pretty small."

At the far end of the ER tent a cluster of nurses and techs orbit a group of stretchers. Bill is in charge as SOD tonight and stands at the foot of the beds, surveying the scene. Dried blood and cast plaster stain the front of his pant legs. His arms are folded in disgust.

"What's up Bill?"

"There are some real scumbags out there," he says shaking his head. "We got a whole burned-up family here. The father is Iraqi National Guard, and sometime earlier tonight, some asshole insurgent threw an incendiary device through the front window of his home. He burned the mother and two daughters. That one is two weeks old, and mostly got it on the face. I haven't intubated her yet because she seems to be crying okay."

The baby is seared across the entire left side of her face, the upper edges of her cheek covered in dry, yellow scabs. From her high-pitched sobbing it is clear she is in great pain, but I am comforted to see that she bleeds easily as the nurse

time in the hospital—and there will be scars—but the girls have a chance to recover fully. "For Leila in particular, it will take many operations and a long time in the hospital for her to survive."

Captain Abbas shakes my hand soberly with his own burned one. "Thank you for your help, doctor." Shortly afterward, he gathers up his men and departs the hospital.

A week later the mother and two-week-old girl Noor are doing well. Their facial burns have healed quickly and I can see shiny pink skin growing to cover the places where their blisters peeled off. Leila has come as far as she can. But now comes the tough part. I will remove the dead skin on her legs and lower torso and graft on healthy skin harvested from unburned parts of her body. It will probably be a four-hour operation in a ninety-degree room. Granted, this is what I do. I have trained for years to take care of children. At DC Children's Hospital, I shaved burned skin from hundreds of children, several of them with burn patterns similar to Leila's. Still, I am nervous. On morning rounds, I am only paying half attention to the discussions of the previous night's work. "...The second troop was a Marine from Florida. The shrapnel came in through the gap in his armor at the axilla. There wasn't much hurt in the chest, just some bleeding lung, but below the diaphragm, there must have been ten holes in the gut. I talked to his wife last night, and she should be meeting him tomorrow in Germany..."

I don't hear the rest of his story. As Donny talks, I plan a map of Leila's skin. I can see the patches of skin where I am going to shave off the grafts. With the flesh on the backs of her legs gone and not coming back, I can only hope to get a thin strip or two from the fronts of her thighs. Most of the graft is going to have to come from her belly. The skin above the umbilicus isn't burned, but it is hard to get an even graft from

the softer belly. It's going to be tricky. I'll need everything
prepared, and this hospital isn't designed for pediatric burns.

I usher Leila into the operating room. Her stretcher is
festooned with stuffed animals, toys, little packets of Chee-
tos and other gifts deposited by many of the hospital staff.
Sally, the anesthetist on the case, points a finger at me and
clenches her forehead in mock-scowl. "Take care of my little
angel here. Make sure she doesn't lose too much blood on the
skin grafts." Without waiting for an answer, she starts sing-
ing, "Don't worry/ 'bout a thing," along with Bob Marley on
the iPod speakers in OR 1. Leila is quickly intubated and falls
asleep. She seems small and powerless on an operating table
that usually supports grown adult soldiers. Back in the US,
there would be any number of hospitals and pediatric surgeons that could take care of her, but in central Iraq I am her
only choice. After prepping her from mid-torso down to her
toes with Betadine, we pass her feet through the fenestration
of a sterile drape. This way, without breaking the sterile field,
I can turn her over during the operation to work burns on the
front and back of her body.

The tech helping me, Violet, has many years of burn surgery experience, and I am thankful for her assistance. We
measure Leila's burns and calculate the size of the surface
area affected. Using a long, flat escharotomy knife designed
for shallow incisions, I slice the dead skin off of her burned
legs, leaving the fat and muscle behind. I remind myself as I
flay skin from this little girl's legs that the skin is unhealthy
and will only feed bacteria and hurt her if left intact. Working quickly, Violet sprays fibrin protein solution on the bleeding wounds and covers them in epinephrine-soaked sponges
to reduce hemorrhage. When she has finished I use the air-
powered dermatome to harvest the skin grafts. A tank of
compressed nitrogen oscillates the blade as I shave partial-

thickness patches of healthy skin from the unburned parts of her body.

I lift the transparent bloody ribbons of skin from Leila's body. I try to concentrate only on the leading edge of the vibrating razor, putting the image of her chubby baby face out of my mind. Being careful to leave behind deeper layers so the skin in those areas will grow back. I run the harvested skin through a mesher and score it, so the skin can be stretched like fishnet stockings to cover a broader area of burn. Patch by patch, I begin the long and meticulous task of covering the raw wounds. It will take hours to get this operation done right.

Halfway through the procedure, I hear a familiar and devastating noise: an incoming MASCAL is announced over the hospital loudspeakers. The OR I planned on using for hours has suddenly become a limited resource. One of the nurses comes in and tells us we will be receiving casualties from two suicide VBIEDs (vehicle borne improvised explosive devices), one in Baqubah, and another around the corner in Balad city. The one in Balad was detonated at a police station next door to a school. Many incoming injured are children. From this point forward the trauma czar, surgical oncologist Abe, will be calling the shots. It is his job to choreograph the care of many patients by many doctors and create order out of the chaos. Almost immediately I see him striding into our OR, marching right toward me. "Coppola, end this operation now. We need the room." He is in charge, there are injured on the way, but there is no way I am leaving until we are finished with Leila.

"I've already harvested the skin, I've got to get it on her."

Abe stands in the doorway, staring at me without blinking. "You need to get her out of this OR in the next five minutes;

the helicopters are about to land." He turns to leave without waiting for a reply.

"There is no way in hell I'm throwing her skin away," I tell the nurse. "Get some skin staplers fast." The choice comes to me in an instant. Battlefield support may be military priority, but I feel no doubts in my heart that my highest duty in this moment is to finish this girl's operation.

I prefer to secure children's skin grafts with dissolving sutures, but right now I don't have the luxury of time. Violet and I work quickly to staple the skin grafts to her legs. Neither of us says a word. When the skin is on, we wrap her legs and torso in layers of mineral oil, non-stick dressings, wet sponges, dry sponges, cotton fluffs, and long rolled gauze bandages. She is hustled out of the OR far quicker than I would have wanted, but at least the grafts are on her. As we wheel her NATO gurney to the ICU, I hear the din of approaching Black Hawks. I turn from her bedside and jog to the ER to join the MASCAL.

Two days later Dr. Yusuf makes his weekly visit to our hospital. When I ask if he has any word on the family whose child has an intersex anomaly, he shakes his head sadly. It is unfortunate, but I had already prepared myself for that answer. I hold out hope and spend the rest of the afternoon with him rounding on Iraqi patients, looking for those who are safe enough to transfer to his hospital. We identify two soldiers who are eating and walking on their own and tell the nurses to ready them for the ambulance. Dr. Yusuf asks us in his meandering manner, "We have had difficulties at the hospital in Balad. In January, the government gave us our budget for the year. Alas, the money for bandages has already run out, and we will not get more for nine months. I am very happy to take these patients from you; they will be happy to have more visits from family. I do not wish to trouble you, but we will be able to care for them better if you can spare some bandages for us." Chief of staff Dwight and I help him locate and package supplies that are in critical demand at his hospital. Together we bundle up square dressings and gauze rolls from a stockpile in a CONEX trailer as Dr. Yusuf looks around wistfully at the stacks of gloves, gowns, and sterile sheets. "You Americans run your hospital so well. There are so many people I could help if we were supplied like this. Your people are very generous to help us in this way."

After the patients are loaded into the ambulance with bags of supplies, Dr. Yusuf and I get a chance to sit in the DFAC together and share a meal. He fills me in on his hospital's experience the day of the mass casualty. "We were very close to where the explosion damaged the school. Many children came to us. Most of them only had minor injuries. Three were dead when they arrived." He tells me this calmly, with his usual quizzical smile. I learn more of his history. His medical training has been peripatetic: two different universities in Iraq, and even a year spent in England. At different times he has studied pediatrics, internal medicine, and surgery. I remind myself that with the state of affairs in Iraq a doctor with a mongrel background is better than a purebred that flees. Dr. Yusuf is really rather remarkable. Here is a man who endures a fractured existence, risking his life each week to work in a pharmacy.

When I ask him more about the school bombing he only shrugs. "There is no sense to it. Who can explain what these bandits do? Little makes sense in Iraq now. I wish you could have seen my country before the war. Perhaps soon there will be fewer bombs."

"Hopefully soon there will be none...that is why we are here."

Dr. Yusuf nods in agreement, but there is little hope in his eyes. It frustrates me that he seems so complacent and accepting of the poor state of affairs in Iraq. Yet I am in no position to judge. I don't know why he stays in Balad in the face of such a struggle, and perhaps he does not either, but it is a good thing he has. As we sip hot mint tea in the DFAC, I recount the operations on Leila and the other children on the day of the MASCAL. Dr. Yusuf is simply happy to hear that we had survivors. I may not always understand Dr. Yusuf, but I feel a sense of solidarity with him. Death and suffering have put us squarely on the same side of the conflict.

I up the distance on my daily run to eight miles. The March air feels cool, even under the insulation of my thirty-five pounds of Kevlar armor and ceramic plates. Rain falls on my head and shoulders in big drops. The Iraqi sky, which is usually the soft tan color of desert dust, looms colder and darker. Before long I am soaked to the bone, but comfortable since the moisture cools me more than my physical effort heats me. It is hard to string together eight miles of road on the base without hitting the wire. I get a little nervous each time my path takes me closer to the perimeter. Rather than run along the edge of the base, I turn back to internal streets whenever I reach the fence. I'm sure I'm in no significant danger from the enemy along the perimeter, but I see a number of trucks hydroplane on the muddy streets and slide onto the shoulder where I run and I'm not taking chances. It certainly makes no sense to travel seven thousand miles from home to get hit by a Hummer.

Troops with nothing but time to spend on their long tours to Iraq have personalized many of the drab structures on base. Some of the decorating pays homage to our base's nickname, "Mortaritaville," earned for the many shells the insurgents launch at us. "The Oasis Hotel," barracks for a squadron deployed out of Korea, has a running tally of mortar hits posted at their front gate. One of the logistics tents has a mock-up of an unexploded rocket shell penetrating halfway through its protective sandbags. The large Air Force H6 general housing compound has a *M*A*S*H*-style signpost with boards listing the distances to various home cities of the occupants. A sign on top of this mile marker reads: HELL, 0 MILES. I pass a truck with its name, "The Beast," stenciled on the front bumper. Perhaps the title refers to the driver? Some of the drivers use tape to spell out their names on the windshields. Personally, I think the visibility in a Humvee is so limited I would not squander a spare inch of the view. However, I do have a laugh at the Humvee with FOUR-MONTH BACHELOR proclaimed on its windshield.

I return to my hooch wet and tired but mentally refreshed. The rain pelts the corrugated metal roof of my trailer. My front door leaks. Water runs down the inside of the door from the top, and then drips back out at the bottom leaving a trail on the dusty door.

As I write letters throughout the evening, the rain falls and nourishes little things lying dormant under the mud. I miss my garden. I miss deadheading the roses and looking for a stem to send in to Meredith with the boys, sure to tell them to claim it as their own. I even miss the stubborn little weeds that hide among the thorny roots and suckers. With the recent rains, I have been thinking of planting my own little garden in the sandbags around my hooch. Friends back home often ask me what they can send so I've requested a few packets of seeds. I expect they will arrive soon at the post office in Balad.

# Hello Muddah, Hello Fadduh

I AM STARTING to get the impression that I am attending some bizarre variant of the Sequassen Boy Scout camp in Connecticut my mother sent me to as a child. Each day the same routine of "rise and shine, and give God your glory, glory" precedes an agenda of odd activities. Daily care packages, red or green bug juice in the DFAC, the incessant teasing of colleagues, the long, sweaty nights writing letters home—it all makes this seem less like a war and more like sleepover camp.

Today, St. Patrick's Day in O'raq, began with a ten-kilometer road race. One hundred and twenty intrepid runners turned out for the event. Most were muscular teens brimming with energy, but there were a few aged grisly specimens like myself. We airmen had a meager showing, but I am proud to report that Air Force women took four of the top five times. Either the sun is getting to me, or I have passed some threshold of normal behavior, because I thought it a good idea to run the race in a leprechaun costume that arrived in a care package. I always wondered who the freaks were who wore costumes to road races, and now I know. I ran with a fellow airman from the hospital, and I was very impressed to learn he was a Vietnam vet with a Purple Heart and twenty deployments under his belt. My finishing time was sixty-nine minutes, which seemed slow for only six miles, even accounting the fact I was wearing full armor and a helmet. It turns out many runners were surprised at their long times, so the organizers rechecked the mileage and realized they had actually mapped out a seven mile course, proving once again that "Army Intelligence" is an oxymoron.

I had worked up a good sweat during the race, so I was delighted to hear the pools were open. I say pools, plural, because there is both an indoor and outdoor facility. The jewel is the fifty-meter outdoor pool with three diving platforms. The highest is ten meters, a daunting height from which to stare down at the water and taunt friends. After completing a few small duties at the hospital, I joined Team Huffy at the Army gymnasium and biked the short distance to the pool. Team Huffy is the orthopedic group, plus a few outside riders like myself, taken to mountain bikes. We dropped our gear at the side of the pool and lay out on chaise lounges, slowly basting in the sun. Many tattoos were on display as we watched young soldiers tumble off the ten-meter platform, compensating for what they lacked in technique with fanfare and bravado. I managed a one-and-one-quarter flip off the high dive, which felt as painful as it sounds. As we lay in the sun, with the water drying on our skin in the warm breeze wafting across the central plains of Iraq, I couldn't help thinking that war is hell.

The grand opening of the pools was marked by an afternoon luau and competitions. Sally won a grass skirt in the limbo contest, proving herself master of many skills. I displayed some promise for a future in private practice by winning the treasure dive, collecting forty-two coins from the bottom of the twelve-foot-deep indoor pool. After completing a nine-year residency, you know how to hold your breath and just get the job done.

As for arts and crafts at this summer camp, we unfortunately have no shortage of work in the OR. As usual, our activity comes and goes as swells of helicopters land with injured patients. Tonight we received nineteen patients, ten of whom proceeded to the operating room. The military hospital in Baghdad became so overwhelmed that they diverted their incoming traffic to us. The rhythmic stutter of the arriving, waiting, and departing Black Hawks and Chinooks continuously filled the tents with noise. We no sooner finished one case than it was time to start another. I washed out wounds and removed jagged fragments of shrapnel. I worked with vascular surgeon Brent to repair a severed artery in a policeman's hand. I explored necks for injuries to the blood supply to the brain, and I sewed the ragged shreds of an ear back together. I splinted broken bones with Bill. In the other two operating rooms, it was the same scene, as our team of highly skilled and practiced airmen patched up the handiwork of a suicide bomber.

By the time we finished operating it was nearly time for breakfast. Five of us stumbled out of the hospital and headed for DFAC2. We washed our hands in turn with Fairy brand soap and queued up for runny eggs and sausage links. We ate at long tables and planned our activities for the day and told tales of victories over other groups of campers in competitions.

At last it was time to check if Leila's skin grafts had taken. We brought her back to OR1 to sedate her. Her legs looked disproportionately large with bulky dressings and splints. I peeled back the numerous layers of protective coverings to expose the transplanted skin. The grafts looked a little hastily finished at the corners, but thankfully they were the dusty rose color that indicates newly forming blood vessels. The patches of skin had taken root like pieces of sod on a bare lawn.

On a daily basis I find myself in awe of the body's wondrous capability for recovery in the face of our rough and clumsy meddling. I am reminded of Ambrose Paré's frequent statement in his records of injured French soldiers: *Je le pansai, Dieu le guérit.* I dressed him, God healed him. Little Leila has come a long way since the day her house burned down, and I hope her good progress continues.

# Above the Tigris

MATT, ONE OF THE critical care doctors, calls me over. "Hey Chris, did you hear we admitted a sick three-year-old who needs a medical attendant to get him out of the country?"

"What's going on?" *Why don't I know about this?*

"We're not sure. He's febrile, his liver's swollen, and his clotting factors are all out of whack."

"Sounds like sepsis and DIC. When was his injury?"

"No, no, no, he wasn't injured, he's a medical case."

"Wait, why is he…" *This is Iraq; never ask why.*

"I'm not really sure why he's here. Baghdad had him for a week or so and couldn't figure out what was wrong with him. They decided to send him to Jordan, but after they shipped him here, his visa fell through so he's not authorized to leave the country. That man next to him is his grandfather." Matt points to an elderly man with a bronzed and wrinkled face sitting in a folding chair next to the boy's bed. "He's a sheik."

The old man's luxurious moustache and beard are snow-white and thick. He sits perfectly still, no question on his face, ready to wait an eternity.

*"Masa al-khayr."* I touch my hand to my chest and bow slightly. He returns the gesture with a smile, but stares straight ahead as his white headdress sways across his face.

I move around the bed and examine the child. If he truly is three years old, he is dangerously small for his age, about the size of a one-year-old in the US. His face is so puffy he cannot open his eyes. Running a high fever, his skin is hot to the touch. Everywhere he is marked with scattered broken blood vessels. I listen to the gurgling breath inside his waterlogged lungs and run my hand across his stomach. His spleen and liver are swollen, but I have no idea what is wrong with him.

We change his fluid and ventilation and send for our chief of staff Dwight, an infectious disease expert. In short order he shows up, trailed by Dr. Yusuf. I had forgotten that it was a Wednesday, Dr. Yusuf's visiting day.

"I see you've met Nizar," Dwight says to me. "I'm curious to hear what you think about him." Dwight looks over at the grandfather, raises his eyebrows and speaks carefully, "A very well-respected tribal leader from a city near Baghdad. The hospital commander at the 86th CSH (combat support hospital) in Baghdad told Rocky to help them out any way we can; it will benefit our relationship with the community. That's why the kid's getting special treatment."

The politics don't matter to me so much as seeing if we can help the child. "It looks to me like some kind of sepsis," I say, trying to stay focused on the boy's health. "What do you think is happening to him?"

"I can't figure it out. They tested everything I would've tried in Baghdad. I was thinking congenital liver disease, but I'm not sure."

"He's a little old for that. Did you check the family history?"

"I was going to get a new set of cultures to see if anything grows. Nothing showed up at CSH."

Before Dwight leaves, Dr. Yusuf interrupts with a quiet clearing of his throat. He is standing at the boy's bedside. "If you will permit me, gentlemen, I would like to make a suggestion."

"Of course, go ahead."

He frowns and tugs ponderously at his moustache. "This boy has leishmaniasis."

Dwight and I exchange a knowing glance: Ahh that makes sense. Parasites. The liver is being attacked, but nothing is growing on the cultures. The organism is transmitted by the sandfly, a tiny insect, nearly impossible to see. Incidence has spiked in the Iraqi population since the beginning of the war, owing to an increase in open waste and standing pools of water. Refugee movement, coupled with close living situations, encourages its spread. Like any surgeon (ours is a pathologically competitive breed), I chide myself for overlooking the signs: How did I miss it?

Dr. Yusuf speaks loudly over the noise of the boy's ventilator. "We usually have two or three children with visceral leishmaniasis in our hospital at any given time; but for doctors from the United States, it must be quite rare and difficult to recognize."

I appreciate his generosity in excusing our ignorance. Besides a few cases in travelers, it was nearly unheard of in the US until soldiers began bringing it home from Desert Storm and Operation Iraqi Freedom. There is a common cutaneous form called the "Baghdad Boil," a skin ulcer that can occur anywhere, clothed regions not excluded, where a sandfly has sunk his teeth. That's the good kind, which can usually be treated with a simple procedure. Nizar must have the rare internal form, visceral leishmaniasis—a variety that can spread through the blood and attack the liver.

We have to move fast because with every hour he is getting worse. Dwight knows of two potential medications. One would have to be flown in from Walter Reed in Washington;

and the other, meglumine antimoniate, which is not approved for use in the US, is available in Baghdad. The prospect of going to Baghdad is frightening, but when I look down at the blood vessels boiling on the boy's face all former notions of safety and risk go out the window.

I make a phone call to the CSH Army hospital in Baghdad and arrange for two Army pediatric surgeons to meet us for a patient drop off. The helicopter to transport the child is already en route, so I run home to put on my DCUs and round up some gear. I check out a Beretta M9 from our armory, holster it in my thigh rig. I join the staff in the ICU to gather the necessary medical equipment. Matt has just come off duty and volunteers to accompany me on the transport. This rotation he is working as an intensivist. Early on I noticed that he seemed to recognize, in garbled transmissions over the ER radio, every city in Iraq that the medics came from. When I asked why he knew so much about the country, he told me he had just finished a stint as an ER doctor and had volunteered for a second deployment. Matt is crazy gung ho.

On the helipad, the prop wash sweeps waves of dust over us. The roar of the rotors and the earplugs we wear make verbal communication nearly impossible. Using hand signals, the pilot and helicopter medic direct us to safely approach the Black Hawk from the side. We load Nizar and Sheik Hakim into the helicopter and secure the litter on the rack. Matt and I climb aboard, and the medic slides the cargo bay door closed behind us. Along the flight line to the west, a pale yellow glow traces the outline of the horizon. The increase of the Black Hawk's turboshaft engines is more of a feeling than a noise. The pilot gently lifts the Black Hawk from the helipad, the nose of the helicopter tips down, and rising quickly to altitude, we bank a graceful arc to the right.

Above the base I start to panic as I realize I am leaving my protected little island. For two months now, I have been trapped here, wishing I were anywhere else. But outside of our fences is where people get hurt. Just by getting on the helicopter, I am breaking a promise I made to Meredith not do anything crazy or take any unnecessary risks. My eyes dart from field to field on the ground, searching for hidden threats, snipers waiting to take us out. All I see below is warm light splashing from small mud huts onto dirt clearings—the dark, still surface of the Tigris River winding its way through fields, giving way to streets and widely spaced homes. But the calm cannot be trusted. At any given moment we could be made the unfortunate target of hostile fire from insurgent anti-aircraft gunners. One shot is all it would take.

There is no time to dwell in fear. I have a patient in my care. Nizar is not doing well; the transport ventilator is too strong and slow for his small breaths. He quickly starts to decompensate and the monitor shows a decreasing oxygen level. I switch to a rubber bag-valve device and manually pump in quick, shallow breaths. Roughly one squeeze every two seconds. I watch the oxygen level hover at 80 percent, and then quickly rise back to 100 percent as my efforts start to pay off. But the oxygen tank is not flowing quickly enough to keep the reservoir full on the bag-valve. I turn the tank on full blast to keep up with the demand. It is going to be close; we have just under a half an hour to get to Baghdad before the oxygen runs out.

The pilot flies in complete darkness, using night vision goggles (NVG) to see his instruments and the terrain below us. We keep the cabin dark to reduce our visibility from below. The only light is the orange screen of the monitor tracing out the child's heart rhythm and vital signs. I keep one hand on the ventilation bag and the other on the boy's chest to feel its rise and fall with each breath. Matt flips on a dim blue light, one that will not interfere with the pilot, and gives Nizar a dose of medication. For the first time, Sheik Hakim eyes contain a hint of supplication, a plea for me to save his dying grandson.

I closely monitor the child's breathing as we cross into Baghdad city limits. Row after row of apartment buildings and cars moving sluggishly in traffic pass beneath us. We are now in the US-held Green Zone near the river. I see palaces and the remains of the National Zoo. The chopper turns, maneuvering over Ibn Sina Hospital's landing zone, and softly sinks to touch down. I glance at the gauge on the oxygen tank. The needle hovers just above empty, vibrating with the helicopter's engines.

Two soldiers approach the Black Hawk on a camouflaged ATV. The medic slides open the side bay doors and a wash of cool, dusty night air whipped into a cyclone by the rotors wafts through the cabin. The medic and the ground crew carefully unload the litter as I maintain a rapid pace of breaths with the bag-valve apparatus. Matt stabilizes the oxygen tank, monitor, and other equipment piled on the litter with Nizar. Working in concert, we exit the Black Hawk and load the stretcher onto the back of the ATV for the short trip to the hospital entrance. I grip the breathing tube tightly and hold it against Nizar's face. Matt and Sheik Hakim squeeze into the ATV seats with the soldiers. I kneel over Nizar's stretcher, one hand pumping the bag, the other hand on his chest feeling for the rhythmic rise and fall of each breath.

My efforts to give breaths to the boy become ineffective. I lean in close, my cheek now against his, and with each pump of the bag I hear a gurgling of air leaking out through his saliva. The endotracheal tube has moved only slightly, but in his small body it is enough to lose the proper position. With the breathing tube out, I can no longer fill his lungs with oxygen. The oxygen level I have fought to maintain the entire flight drifts down from 100 percent in tiny steps every time his heart beats. "Get a move on!" I yell at the driver. "I lost his airway."

Inside the compound, we race through concrete barricades to the lobby entrance of the hospital. A tech throws open the doors. I pause my efforts long enough to help move the litter onto a hospital gurney. For an instant, I marvel at the sight of a genuine, padded, four-wheel gurney. I have not seen one for two months in the tent hospital. I climb aboard with Nizar and do my best to puff oxygen into his mouth through a small mask attached to the bag and valve. His oxygen flow is undetectable. His heart has slowed to a dangerous rate. I start compressing his chest in a rapid rhythm with the tips of my fingers, stopping every few seconds for a puff of air.

We rush through the lobby, a tight team pushing the gurney with Nizar on top and me astraddle. In the elevator we endure a painful moment of frozen time as we climb to the second floor. When the doors part, Matt and the tech spring into action and wheel Nizar into the intensive care unit. The ICU nurses bring us the code cart of medications and intubating equipment. Nizar's heart is sputtering, his limbs turning purple. Using the thin metal blade of a laryngoscope I elevate his tongue and jaw, glimpse his vocal cords, and slide a new endotracheal tube into his airway. With a fresh flow of oxygen from the registers on the wall of the ICU, we soon see his oxygen level rise. I call out to the nurse performing CPR, "Hold compressions, and let's check his EKG." His heart rhythm has returned to a normal rate. I feel for a pulse in his neck. It is there, bounding and strong, amplified by the atropine and epinephrine we have given him. He is going to make it.

I sigh in exhaustion and then turn to the ICU doctor. "His airway's intact and he's got a strong carotid pulse. He's all yours." Matt and I collapse into the bright orange stackable plastic chairs at the foot of the bed. Our job is done. With a new breathing tube Nizar can get the oxygen he needs. As the boy's circulation strengthens and his little feet turn from purple to pink, expressions of relief finally begin to spread across the faces of the team. Nurses and techs buzz around his bed, tidying up his lines and going over his body from head to toe. His vital signs return to normal, and the respiratory therapist connects him to the mechanical ventilator. When the ICU staff takes over, I explain to Sheik Hakim what has happened. Listening to the translator's Arabic, he wordlessly waves a hand at me, smiles, and bows his head.

Built in the 1960s by four Iraqi doctors, Ibn Sina is a storied place, named for the greatest of Islamic physicians, Abu Ali al-Hussain ibn Abdallah ibn-Sina, known in the West as Avicenna. Abu Ali was born in 981 CE in what is now Uzbekistan. He traveled to Iran where he wrote a medical encyclopedia, the Qanun (the Arabic word for "law"). In four volumes, the Canon of Medicine is over a million words long and was translated into Latin for use throughout Europe. After Saddam Hussein took over the hospital in the nineties, it became the private hospital for his family and the Ba'athist elite. Now the four-story structure houses the 86th CSH Army Hospital in the heart of Baghdad's Green Zone. As I look around, it is clear that the workmanship is sloppy and the building poorly constructed. The marble floors are beautiful slabs, but they have been slapped together with irregular seams spaced by jagged gaps. The intricate golden trim is nailed to panels of unevenly stained plywood. Still, after operating in a tent for two months, walking through marbled halls under high ceilings feels like a bit of a spectacle.

Looking at the spacious structure and numerous modern amenities available to the Ibn Sina team, I cannot help but swell with pride for our crew in Balad. We match them pace for pace with our dusty little cluster of tents and CONEX containers. "Can you believe that we're the neurosurgery center for the theater?" I ask Matt as we make our way through the halls. "They send troops with busted-up heads from this spanking-clean hospital to us so we can open their skulls in a shipping container."

"It's like Dwight says, 'It's not about the tents, it's about the people.'"

His response is typical. Matt is a laid-back, optimistic character, never fazed by the changes that roll our way. I think the main reason he volunteered to help with the child was to visit a new arena, and I appreciate his easy company and low-key surfer's vibe as the two of us wander the hospital curiously eyeing everything and everyone like two kids on a class field trip.

After a few minutes, we stumble upon an all too familiar sight: the burn unit, where two young girls are recovering on stretchers. The scene instantly reminds me of Balad. Surrounded by their parents and other doctors, the girls lie bandaged and covered in blankets, their faces and upper bodies singed with dark crisp scars. The only difference here is a clean floor, well-padded ICU beds, and spacious patient rooms. Sadly, my friends at this hospital tell me that even with the amenities they have had the same difficulty keeping malnourished Iraqi children alive after serious injury.

The girls' parents shake our hands and say *shukran*, expressive of their gratitude, while the girls appraise us quietly from their beds. They rest comfortably, well cared for by the nursing staff; and for a moment I recognize in them Noor and Leila's same courageous spirit. I plan an early morning check-up of Leila's skin grafts, staying optimistic, resisting the urge to be envious of modern conveniences I don't have.

We finally make it back to the hospital lobby, but the Black Hawk that brought us here has already departed on its return trip to Balad. The next flight won't leave till dawn. Upon hearing the news, my eyes pop open wide and I look to Matt for his reaction. He busts out laughing and says, "Just roll with the changes, baby!"

We learn that there is an MWR facility in the basement of the hospital and decide to explore. Downstairs we meet three off-duty troops who are part of the security detachment that patrols the hospital. They are just hanging out—all three seem incredibly young, fresh out of high school. They would look less out of place loitering outside a Hot Topic clothing shop in a suburban San Antonio mall. "Tallboy," a thin, lanky curtain rod of a soldier, at least six-and-a-half feet tall, balances precariously on top of a patio chair that wobbles with each sway of his jittering knees. His uniform hangs loosely off his body, and his long thin wrists stretch out from the cuffs. "Dang it!" he cusses in a Texas drawl as he struggles to tape a plastic sheet over a small rectangular window near the ceiling. "Mischief" laughs at him from his comfortable spectator's post, sprawled out across two chairs with his unlaced boots propped up on the folding table that supports the TV. He wears a camouflage bandana around his reflective bald head and has a cigarette wedged behind his ear. "Big Mama" is a short, thickly built Latina who stands behind Tallboy with her arms folded, barking out criticisms and asking him what kind of idiot his mother raised him to be. Her hair is pulled back in a severe and shining bun, and it is clear she is the leader of the group. As Matt and I enter the room, Big Mama straightens her back and says, "Good evening, sirs."

Mischief flashes a peace sign over his shoulder and calls out, "Welcome to the VIP lounge, sirs!"

Maybe it is just a characteristic of medics, but there is an instant reaction upon walking into any room to help in the most efficient way possible. So when Matt and I see Tallboy up on the chair, we quickly join him. I stabilize the shaking chair and brace my arm against his leg. Matt begins tearing off measured strips of duct tape and handing them up to Tallboy. Once we have a rhythm going, Matt asks him, "So what are you doing up there, anyway, dude?"

"There's a whole mess of feral cats on the streets and they keep sneaking in through the broken window. We're taping up the windows and holes in the wall so they can't get in and fuckin' steal our food. Oh! Pardon me, sirs."

Big Mama chimes in from her position as foreman, "It's a good thing you got here to keep Lurch from busting his head open."

Tallboy finishes securing the breach and jumps from the chair in a flurry of limbs. We nod at each other approvingly as we dust our hands off. Mischief calls over, "What channel do you want to watch, sirs? There's AFN, or we can get Al Jazeera if you want a little of that 'Lalalalalala' stuff." For a moment, he ululates in a shrill tone. Then he chuckles and says, "Grab some snacks and drinks if you want 'em."

We settle in with the trio on an assortment of threadbare couches and La-Z-Boy recliners. They share stores of cashews and Pringles with us while we watch badly-scripted social announcements on Armed Forces Network that admonish us to refrain from criticizing high-level members of the government and to keep an eye on our battle buddy for signs of suicidal behavior. The soldiers seem bored, and I feel for them—just regular Americans doing their best to get through a deployment that is much longer than our little four-month tour. They have done their best to make this little lounge their peaceful oasis. Now they share their hoarded treats with Matt and me as freely as if we were brothers. Big Mama continues to scold as Mischief tries to get us involved in his taunting of Tallboy, who laughs it off, content in the company of trusted comrades. Eventually, Mischief convinces Big Mama to show us a picture of her daughter; and with a wave of pride breaking over her face she announces, "This is my beautiful baby; she's with her grandparents in Tampa."

For a few minutes, we coo and admire the picture of her baby. Soon the transportation sergeant enters with news of our ride. She has found a helicopter pilot willing to bring "medical equipment" back to Balad. Matt and I bid farewell.

We leave Ibn Sina hospital a few short hours after arriving. As we fly back to Balad in darkness, the isolating noise of the helicopter seems to hold time still. On the surface of the Tigris the reflection of the moon shimmers as it dances, charting the course we follow north to our temporary home. I compose in my mind an e-mail to Meredith. I realize I have broken my promise not to leave the base. Now I have to confess and assure her that I have returned safely. That will not be easy.

# Twelve Hour Sleep

AT THE STROKE of midnight it is Easter in Balad. Midnight chow is up, so I hoof it the quarter mile to DFAC 2. The place is brimming with hungry troops and decorated to the hilt. Even the cafeteria line is a carnival of decorations, the most remarkable ones carved from fruits artificially tinted with food coloring. Eggs and streamers hang from the low ceiling. Tables are arranged tavern-style with pastel purple paper and Easter centerpieces. Situated on one of the tables is a custard Golgotha, complete with three lime crosses hidden behind scraggly-armed trees made of bread. The *piéce de résistance* is a tiny, watermelon rind Jesus, crucified with toothpicks onto a bas-relief cross carved into a second watermelon.

I appreciate the effort, but weird, brightly colored decorations don't make me forget I am stuck celebrating Easter in a war zone. Frankly, any inclusion of religion in this God-awful mess is an insult. I try to keep an open mind and look at both sides, but I fail to see how "Muslim extremists" are any different than extremists of other religions. The Muslims I meet every day at the hospital are just like me, more concerned about the health and happiness of their families than any holy war. We laugh and coo in the faces of happy babies as if we were all cut from the same cloth.

The Easter bonanza offers no antidote for my poor sleeping habits. I return to my hooch to find my old friend insomnia waiting up for me. My problem is that I still retain the rhythms of home. So many moments in the day, I glance at the time on my pager and imagine what Meredith and the boys are doing. At first I tried getting up early to force an early bedtime. When that didn't work, I toyed with da Vinci sleep, napping for thirty minutes every four hours. I have also tried reversing my sleep/wake cycle since I am staying up every night anyway. Nothing has worked; insomnia has become my battle buddy in the past two months and shows no sign of leaving soon.

I get called into rounds at 0800. I haven't slept all night, but somehow being alone in my hooch writing letters has cleared my mind and refreshed my defenses for another day of work. As our group of surgeons passes from bed to bed, I remember each patient according to which of their principal organs has been shattered. In the first bed is the Iraqi policeman whose left leg is held on by a lattice of carbon rods and a few fragile blood vessels. At the end of the tent is the Iraqi civilian woman, mother to one of our interpreters, who has a series of fistulas leaking bile from her intestines. Next we come to the Iraqi policeman I met my first night on call. He lies in a drug-induced stupor, as the ventilator pumps his lungs in regular intervals. His belly has been closed, but several rubber tubes sprout from his skin: some to drain leaking intestinal fluids, and two to feed him a liquid-like baby formula. The surface of his eyes is coated with an ointment to prevent infection and keep them from drying out through his unblinking days. It is hard to imagine him as the virile twenty-two year old he was before he was shot. At least he hasn't died.

I break off from the pack to operate with Donny, who is busy washing out a man's abdomen. The man was admitted to the hospital before we arrived in January and has endured more than thirty operations. I do not know his name, but we call him "Brando" because his long illness has caused his face to swell up so that his puffed cheeks resemble Don Vito Corleone's. The man was injured attempting to protect us from a suicide bomber driving a truck full of explosives toward the wire. I feel callous calling him a stupid nickname, but without it he would be nothing more than a number. Hopefully, one day he will regain consciousness—it would be a true victory to learn his name and find his family. Today, we are just hoping to remove the dressing from his open abdomen and clean his injured intestine.

Even though I'm tired, operating feels better than trying to sleep. For some reason, staring at an open wound bounded by a field of sterile blue towels brings me comfort. Donny must have noticed the raspy sound of my voice because he asks me if I have a cold. I try to shrug it off, but from the top of the table, where she is giving the patient anesthetic, Sally hears me coughing and peeks over the screen of sterile sheets that separates the operative field from her anesthesia area. "He's right. You sound like crap, babe."

"It's just the 'Balad Crud,' a little cough courtesy of the burn pit. Plus, I haven't been sleeping too well. Aren't you supposed to stay on your side of the drapes?"

"I don't know what you're complaining about, it seems a lot cleaner up here than in that abdomen," Sally answers, as her head dips back below the screen to monitor the anesthesia cart.

Donny pulls down his blue facemask. "Chris, take care of yourself. You've got to settle in for the long haul over here. After we finish with Brando, why don't you head out and catch a nap."

We rinse the intestines with warm, sterile saline. Fortunately, there are no dead or leaking loops of intestines, but his organs are still too swollen to close his abdomen, so we place layers of non-adherent plastic and an absorbent sponge over his skin to seal the wound. An electric vacuum is attached to draw moisture out of his abdominal cavity until it is time for the next washout in two days. I leave Brando in the capable hands of Donny and Sally and head back to my hooch.

A dirty pile of socks, underwear, and black T-shirts still sits in front of my locker, and a stack of unanswered letters awaits me on my cot. I missed Mass this morning, but that is nothing new. Duties at the hospital have prevented me from attending any of the Holy Week ceremonies. It wasn't the first time since becoming a surgeon that I worshiped in my own way, at a slightly more intimate altar in the OR. Growing up, we celebrated any big Catholic holiday with our aunts, uncles, and grandparents over a big Italian meal. The Easter message made a lot more sense to me gathered around the dinner table with loved ones. But in Iraq, it's different; seeing so much killing in the name of God poisons the message of loyalty, beneficence, and brotherhood. The mild cold symptoms I have felt the last few days are probably just psychosomatic. Proof I'm sick of being here.

Yet, after another poor night of sleep, I get up and do it all over again. One man needs a short but challenging re-operation for a recurrence of a groin hernia. He is a young

US soldier Bill found in clinic this week. I use a technique called a "plug and patch," strengthening the weak area in the muscle by inserting a mesh that looks a lot like the material in a screen window. We have no factory-made plugs over here, so I build one from a flat piece of sterile mesh. The final product looks like a badminton shuttlecock.

When the operation is complete and the anesthesia has worn off, the man wakes up disoriented, his head lolling from side to side. For a moment he gazes bug-eyed around the room, then fixes his eyes on Sally and reaches both arms out for a hug. "There, there," she says, flashing one of her cheerful grins and winking at me over his shoulder. "It's all going to be okay. You're just a big sweet teddy bear, aren't you?" Maybe it is the lack of sleep, but my heart swells for this dear, quirky, compassionate woman. I have no doubt I am with family when she says to me, "Guess what, if you get an operation, you'll get a hug too."

I shuffle back to my temporary home and climb into bed. The display on my pager by my head reads 11:00 AM. I plan to sleep eight hours and wake in the evening to stay up all night. Two hours later I open my bleary eyes to the afternoon sun streaming through the shutters. The time stamp on my pager indicates it has been going off for half an hour.

I'm in the ER in minutes. I see three young American soldiers wheeled in, trails of blood splashing across the floor as the grim medics rush past the line of beds in the ER. There is blood flowing from the soldiers' limbs, blood seeping through the mesh fabric of the NATO litters, blood everywhere. Abe and Bill quickly go to work. One soldier soon has large IVs in each arm and is receiving an emergency transfusion. The team pulls off the tatters of his clothing and examines him for wounds. One leg is severely damaged, with shards of shattered bone visible; the other leg has several gaping wounds where bleeding muscle shows through bare, pulverized flesh.

The next man looks good, a little shaken up, but awake and strong with good color. I look him in the eyes and ask, "What's your name?"

"Adams, sir." His left leg is injured. A fragment of metal entered the thigh on the outside and came so close to shooting out of the inner surface I can see it bulging under the skin. It was so heated from the explosion of their Hummer that a patch of burned skin marks its location. I lift his leg and he cries out, flinching. His femur is broken. I splint the bone, give him some IV fluid, and move on to the third man.

The nurses and techs have already undressed him and started an IV catheter. He is hurting but talking. This man is the Hummer commander, in charge of the vehicle when it hit the IED. He used to be a tanker; and after the way his vehicle got shredded today, I bet he wishes he still was. All three soldiers look like they are barely out of their teens. He asks me, "How are my men, Doc?" I tell him I've just come from Adams and he is doing well. He responds, "They are both named Adams." I lie and tell him they are going to be fine.

He is worried that the first Adams in trauma bay II is going to lose an eye; I'm concerned he is going to lose his life. For the moment, it is best to let him think that. It may be the only way he will keep his calm.

I look over the commander's injuries. A fragment of Hummer the size and shape of a Swingline stapler is embedded in his right arm. The flesh is torn away, and I can see the shiny ends of his bones where the elbow joint has broken open. At the scene of the injury, this man applied a tourniquet to his own shoulder and then crawled to where the first Adams lay bleeding to death. With his good arm, he tightened tourniquets around both of Adams' thighs. He then kept talking to the soldier while waiting for the Black Hawks to arrive. I give him morphine while putting him through the painful task of removing his uniform sleeve from around the embedded chunk of metal. As the powerful narcotic takes effect, I see his pupils constrict. His speech slows and his responses become drawn. As I work he winces weakly, but I can see that he is protected from the worst of the pain.

Abe is in charge as the trauma czar. He motions to the first Adams and directs, "Get him to the OR and take his leg off." Adams needs an amputation of the left leg, and the wounds on the right leg cleaned. I hurry him into the OR, turn care of the Hummer commander over to vascular surgeon Brent, and get ready to amputate the soldier's leg. I have performed amputations since I was a surgical intern. Often they were on aging veterans who suffered gangrene. The operations were scheduled, and it was apparent to everyone, including the men, that the rotten leg was doing them no good. Amputation was a chance to get rid of a festering infection and shuttle the patients out of the hospital quickly and in better health. However, I have yet to perform an amputation at Balad. Orthopedic surgeons perform most of them, but these patients came in so fast and critically ill the orthopedics had not yet arrived at the hospital.

Looking down at this young man's muscular legs, I see his left leg is blown apart above the knee, attached only by a strip of skin and gristle. I take out a set of shears, exactly like the one I keep in my kitchen to quarter chickens, and cut his leg off with two snips.

Larry lends a hand and together we move the man to the table, leaving his destroyed leg behind on the litter. After his skin is prepped with iodine, I find the stumps of severed arteries in his thigh and stop the bleeding. Working quickly and methodically, Larry and I cut away dead chunks of muscle and crack off the sharp shards of his thighbone until the cut end is short and smooth. Sally keeps him alive by pumping blood and warmed fluids into his IV catheters. We clean the wounds on his right leg and identify his broken right femur. When orthopedic surgeon Tom arrives I help him use pins and graphite bars to stabilize the broken right thighbone with an external scaffold.

While we operate, Brent brings the Hummer commander with the injured arm to a second table in the OR. Soaked in blood, the tourniquet pinches into his bicep, and metal shards and ends of broken bone jut from the bloody tissue at his elbow. His hand belongs on a corpse. He has held onto his responsibility as long as possible. From his NATO stretcher, he has watched over his men like a hawk, inquiring after their status and directing care to them whenever he could. But now the morphine and Versed are starting to submarine his will. The cords of muscle in his face and neck relax, and he reclines fully for the first time since arriving. As his eyes lose their focus, he suddenly seems much younger, like the recent high school graduate he is. His cheeks and lips soften; his eyelids gently close. Stripped of his uniform and intubated for surgery, he no longer appears to be a toughened commander— just a young kid in a deep dreamless sleep. This soldier who saved the life of the man on the table in front of me needs to have his arm amputated. We cut it off.

Bloody and sweaty, we clean their wounds and wrap their limbs in dressings. All three men survive, and we wheel them to the intensive care unit to await evacuation to Germany.

I suppose I could state the obvious. I thank God these brave men survived what could have been lethal injuries. I am proud that the assembled expertise at our hospital made the difference between sending home corpses in flag-draped boxes and sending home three heroic men with their whole lives ahead of them. Still, I want it over now. Why can't the last death really be the last death?

On my way back to the hooch, I find Larry setting up the recreation tent for movie night. He wishes me a happy Easter.

"It's good to see you, but it doesn't much feel like Easter away from family," I say to him.

"Well, I was thinking that too, but Christ is with us no matter where we are. Have you seen the plants starting to grow in the fields outside the base? It's a sign of rebirth. We had a wonderful celebration mass today."

I may not share the conviction of his religious beliefs, but I appreciate the sentiment. We are in this together. I trust these people. I know they can turn in the goods; I see them do it day after day. They work miracles with duct tape and 550 Cord when things fall apart. They gently hold the hands of dying men and sometimes snatch them back from the brink. When I stumble, they catch my elbow. When I sink into a funk they tease me back into a good mood. They give me chocolate to keep the Dementors away.

# Sad News

March 24, 2005

Dear Friends,

I have been caring for a two-year-old girl with burns named Leila for the past month. In spite of heroic efforts from the team of doctors, nurses, and techs taking care of her, she passed away tonight at 1850. I knew her long enough to learn that her favorite stuffed animal was a pink bear, she loved chips and snacks, and her giggles brought joy to her mother and father. Nearly everyone in our hospital from the ER, OR, ICU, wards, respiratory, pharmacy, nutrition, laboratory—even the chaplain—has had a hand in this sweet girl's treatment. It is only through the hard work of those caring people that she was able to survive as long as she did.

For the past four days, she has been critically ill on life support. Her young heart gave out after enduring much more than one with less will to live could have withstood. We cleaned her and wrapped her in pads and a blanket. Her parents were unable to visit today due to heightened security on the base, so we contacted her father's military unit, and our guards arranged for him to pass through security this evening. One of our ambulance medics picked him up at the gate along with Leila's older brother and her uncle. Kasim helped me speak to them, but there was little to say. I carried Leila out to the ambulance. After the men in her family climbed in, I placed her in her uncle's arms. I lost sight of them as the Humvee ambulance doors swung shut.

If you pray, please remember Leila's family in your prayers. Thank you for all your prayers for Leila and the toys and treats you sent. She is not the first child I have seen die, and I know I am not so fortunate that she will be the last. Tomorrow, I will go back to work and try to help the others who come my way. But tonight I am broken.

I will write again soon.

Yours, Chris

# Abu Ghraib

ON APRIL 2, 2005, we receive casualties from the Battle of Abu Ghraib. Insurgents and prisoners launched a coordinated attack on the infamous detention facility, located twenty miles west of Baghdad, which began with vehicle borne IEDs to cut off the entrance roads, effectively trapping the Marines inside the wire. They followed with a two-hour barrage of bullets, grenades, rockets, and mortars. At one point, a suicide bomber drove a truck packed with explosives up to the wall. Marines engaged the vehicle with M-16 fire, and it detonated too far away to breach the gates. The thirty-four hundred prisoners inside the facility then took to rioting, throwing rocks and swinging makeshift clubs at the military police officers. Eventually they broke through a fence, but the police battalion held them back. Incoming rocket and mortar fire injured fighters on each side. I am grateful none of them died in the attack.

The wounded were first evacuated to Ibn Sina hospital in Baghdad. Those who required further treatment were sent on to our hospital. Both facilities are set up for combat support surgery, but we have the lion's share of the subspecialists. All soldiers requiring neurological, ophthalmologic, and ENT (ear, nose, and throat) surgery eventually come to us. The first patient I receive in the ER is a stocky man, with a fuzzy red crew cut and chubby cheeks covered in a riot of freckles. He looks to be at least thirty years old, older than our usual patients. Wrapped in a thick vinyl body bag for warmth, he is covered except for his distended belly, which bears a bulky white dressing covering a long incision. The bandage is marked in black Sharpie, SMALL BOWEL INJURY, PRIMARY REPAIR, 2 APR. Drifting in and out of consciousness from a whirlwind day of emergency surgery and a helicopter evacuation, his eyes spin crazily as he tries to focus on my face. I speak to him in loud, measured tones. "Sir, you are at the hospital in Balad. Can you hear me?"

He responds in short bursts, gasping for a breath every two or three words. "Rogers, how's Rogers? After the mortar hit, I had to drag him out. I couldn't keep him awake. I thought he might have increased ICP (intracranial pressure)."

"Rogers is here; he is fine. You flew in together on the same Black Hawk. He is across the tent from you. Can you see him?" I lift his head so he can see Rogers resting across the ER, sedated with morphine and Versed, but doing well.

"Is he awake? I can't see from here."

"My partner has been talking with him, he's okay. You both needed surgery in Baghdad for shrapnel injuries, but he's doing well now."

"I'm a Corpsman. I tried to get him out."

"I know. You did well."

A Navy Corpsman is one of the most versatile medical providers in the world. With a high school diploma and a couple hundred hours of training, they perform the brunt of the medical work in the Navy. Corpsmen who serve with the Marines complete an additional seven weeks of training at Camp Lejeune, North Carolina. A motivated Corpsman can do about as much for an injured troop with his medical bag and pockets as I can do with a whole hospital. During World

War II, Pharmacist's Mate Wheeler Lipes saved a sailor's life by performing an emergency appendectomy in the mess hall of a submarine cruising under the surface of the Pacific.

The red headed Corpsman I am treating tended to his men with little regard for his own safety or injuries. During the attack, he rushed to the scene of a mortar blast to evacuate the wounded. When another mortar fell he took shrapnel to the body; flak penetrated his belly and tore through his intestine. Through it all, he continued to care for his men. If he had not revived Rogers and dragged him to safety, he would have bled to death or suffocated under the debris. Looking at this brave medic, I ask myself whether I could I have displayed the same courage. I don't have an answer. All I can conclude is that his injuries will require the removal of a portion of his intestines.

Another Marine's injuries are so severe he has lost both of his eyes. We receive him intubated with a bloody gauze roll wrapped around his head. When we remove the dressing, all that is left of his face above the lips is a torn up jigsaw puzzle of scorched flesh. His eye sockets hold a pulp of blood and ruptured sclera, and the white edges are crushed into bits like the remains of broken eggshells. We bandage his face and he is hustled off to the CT scanner to see if his brain is bleeding or swelling. Our team fans out to check wounds, patch them up, and bundle the troops for their journey up-range, leaving their care in the able hands of the physicians in Germany and their fates in the more able hands of God.

As the casualties come in, I move the pediatric patients to a separate ward to give them and their parents an oasis away from the chaos of wounded soldiers. For days Bill has been teasing me that I have a secret intention of opening a children's hospital in Balad. "You claim to be a pediatric surgeon, but I think you are just a pediatrician with a knife." He asks me if I'm developing a good referral pattern from the local doctors for my new private practice. One morning there is even a sign tacked up in the hospital tent that reads, THE COPPOLA HOSPITAL FOR THE BETTERMENT OF IRAQI CHILDREN FOUNDATION, INC. It's a good laugh, but I honestly don't know if the sign was hung out of annoyance or admiration. Whatever the intent, I hope I can live up to that challenge in some small way.

As I gaze over the mess of mangled Marines, Kasim approaches in agitation. He folds his arms across his chest and speaks in frustration. "You know this place Abu Ghraib will never be good for anything. The people hate it too much. When Saddam put our people in there they disappeared. Mothers would beg for years to know if their sons were still alive. These things that happened with the American soldiers torturing prisoners at Abu Ghraib, this was nothing new for Iraqis. It was always that way at Abu Ghraib. Only insurgents and Americans would fight over such a place. You should destroy it. Nothing good will come of it."

Like the rest of our country, I was horrified last year when pictures of prisoner abuse by US troops surfaced. The Iraqis were not so surprised; they assumed that such things were happening. The mass graves beyond the prison attest to the fact that far worse happened under Saddam Hussein. But that offers little solace to me. Torture is torture.

We move through the ER and over to my makeshift pediatric ward. Mothers tend to their children, tidying up blankets and propping pillows. Fathers pace the floor, anxiously awaiting news from a doctor. "You know these people are very lucky to have you caring for their children. It is very hard to find a doctor on the outside these days."

"Well, I know parents feel the same way about their kids that I feel about mine."

"Your rotation will be over soon and you will leave. Do you think you will ever return to Iraq?"

I don't know how to answer him. I hate what has happened in this country and I hate having to see it every day. Most of all, I hate being away from Meredith and our sons. When I am back in her arms, the last thing I would ever want to do is come back to this hole.

"I will be in the Air Force for another four years. Unless the war ends soon, I guess I will be back."

"Then that will be good for us."

Kasim and I seldom have good news for each other. Still, I appreciate his company. Sometimes I wonder what will happen to him after I leave. I know I will miss him.

As the days go by, the trickle of children becomes a steady flow. Each time one arrives at the ER, I am summoned from my hooch to look the child over. One day we receive a little girl named Farrah with an obstructed liver. She and her parents come to us from a nearby village, worried about her poor growth and weakness. Farrah is a diminutive eighteen-month-old girl with severe jaundice. Around her irises, her sclerae have been stained from natural white to a nearly fluorescent yellow; her malnourished hair has the color of sun-dried straw. She doesn't walk or crawl, but her upper body is always in motion, swinging a toy, clapping, and reaching for her mother.

Her mother and father are constantly at her side. Her father dresses in a pair of brown corduroys and a plaid short-sleeve button-down shirt. Her mother wears the standard black *abaya*, but leaves her face unveiled and stained with eye make-up. The two parents alternate speaking, orating in almost perfectly harmonized two-part lyrics as they relate their daughter's medical history and describe her illness, a textbook case of biliary atresia.

The rare congenital illness causes a blockage of the liver and is fatal before age five if not treated with the Kasai procedure—a surgical connection between the intestine and liver, which bypasses the blocked bile ducts. I usually perform the operation before the child is three months old, but Farrah is already eighteen months and showing signs of advanced liver damage. The procedure at this late age gives her only a one-in-five chance of success. I first look for resources at Iraqi hospitals, but Dr. Yusuf and I do not find any Iraqi surgeons willing to undertake her care. That comes as no surprise. The local hospitals can barely keep up with the daily incoming tide of injured civilians. I consult pediatric surgeons around the world in an online discussion group, and the consensus is that the Kasai is worth a try.

Farrah's father, well-spoken and sharp, worked as an engineer before the war, and his wife has an equally quick, analytic mind. They hear me out patiently as I explain to them that I usually treat biliary atresia near birth and, at the age of eighteen months, the odds are stacked against us. I tell them that the operation, which is dangerous in itself, only has a one-in-five chance of giving her a lifelong cure.

"What other choice do we have?" the father asks.

"You always have the choice to do nothing. If we do nothing we avoid the risk of the operation, but her disease will not stop. I can't see the future for Farrah any more than you can, but I can tell you that doctors around the world have found that biliary atresia will eventually kill every child who is not treated. Most will die by age two."

They have other questions for me, and, answering them in turn, I carefully explain how I will make an incision across the top of the belly, with the goal to suture a loop of intestine to an opening at the base of the liver, so the bile will have a detour around the scarred passage through the biliary duct.

They demonstrate an understanding of the operation that is
clearer than some medical students I have known. Eventually, they look at each other in agreement, the communication
of loved ones passing wordlessly between their eyes, and Farrah's father says, "We would like you to do the operation."

I commit myself to treating her in our hospital. As I make
arrangements for the operation, I am surprised to find resis-
tance from a few members of the hospital staff. Thus far the
other doctors and nurses have posed no opposition to my care
of the many sick children who come through our door. But
Farrah's case is different. It is an elective procedure, and a
conscious choice to dedicate our resources to her care. When
our chief of staff, Dwight, warns that I cannot jeopardize the
care of our troops, I promise him I will only start the operation when the OR is empty and five spaces are ready and waiting for an emergency.

In the ICU, several of the nurses have gathered around
nurse commander Diana. As I enter, they quickly disperse,
busying themselves organizing charts and supplies. Diana
pulls me aside, "Chris, my nurses want me to bring up an
issue with you. There are rumors going around that you're
going to try an experimental surgery on a child, and they just
aren't prepared to handle it. You have to understand that a lot
of these nurses never have any contact with pediatric patients
back home. It really isn't fair to put this extra demand on
them."

The rumors have magnified the danger and threat of my
operation, but I am happy to see Diana sticking up for her
nurses. I tell her, "The Kasai procedure is rare, but it certainly isn't experimental. It will be a lot less stressful on this
child than the multiple fragment wounds we treat every day."

I summon the nurses and speak to them as a group. "I'm
happy you brought this up. I know you are concerned because

you want what's best for this child. But I also know that you can do it. I see you care for these kids every day. If it makes any difference, I'll promise to stay by Farrah's side in the ICU as she recovers. I just ask you to give me a chance to help this little girl." The nurses nod quickly and agree to go along with the operation. I think they were prepared to help all along but wanted to see that I would keep up my side of the bargain.

I have a much tougher time with the anesthesiologists. None of them is comfortable with a patient of this size, and they tell me they will not participate in her case. The head anesthesiologist Stan says bluntly, "There is no way this operation is happening here. It's incredibly inappropriate for you take on this non-combat related operation on a child—we're a hospital for injured troops, first and foremost."

"We take care of blown up and burned up kids this size every day. She is a child in need, it isn't any different."

"End of discussion!" and he storms out of the OR.

Sally, sitting in a corner trying to make a call home, watches the entire episode. She puts the phone down. "Chris, I was going to do the case for you. I told Stan if he wasn't woman enough to do it to move over and let me do the job. A couple of us wanted to help you, but he forbid it. You know I'd do it for you, Hon, but he gave me a direct order."

"Thanks, Sally, it means a lot."

"If it was my kid, I'd want someone to go to bat for her."

"What the hell am I going to do?"

"Don't worry, you'll figure it out. I know you, Chris."

I catch a break when an Army pediatric surgeon I know in Baghdad e-mails me with the good news that he knows a pediatric anesthesiologist stationed at the 228th CSH at Camp Speicher, near Tikrit to the north. Like me, pediatric anesthesiologist Drew is a specialist deployed to care for combat-injured troops. I call Tikrit on the Army/Navy portable radio. After several false starts with privates and sergeants, a man comes on the wire and says, "AOD here."

"This is Major Coppola, a surgeon at the Air Force Theater Hospital in Balad. By any chance do you have a pediatric anesthesiologist named Drew assigned to your hospital?"

"Sure do, you're talking to him."

"I've got a rather strange request: I'm a pediatric surgeon and I'm taking care of an eighteen-month-old girl with biliary atresia. Our anesthesiologists won't put her asleep. Do you think you could come down here to anesthetize her for a Kasai?"

"A Kasai in Iraq? Seriously? I get off duty at 1700. I can try to catch the rotator in after dark."

And this is how it usually goes with doctors who specialize in children. When we are taking care of adults, we look for any chance to do what we were made for.

I stop by the MCC to let Abe know I am setting up the case. The last thing he needs as the trauma czar is to have some surprise sprung on him in the OR. I find him in the command tent hanging out with Bill and Brent. It is almost dinnertime and they are getting ready for the regular surgeon family dinner trip to the DFAC. When he sees me enter he gets the first word, "Chris, I had a little talk with Stan about your girl."

"Sorry about that, sir, I meant to come tell you myself, but I've been busy tracking down a pediatric anesthesiologist."

"I know. Stan came in here and told me that he runs the OR, and he doesn't want the case going, even if you did find an anesthesiologist to do it."

"Well, I got one, and he's on his way tonight. Sir, I know we can get this kid through the operation."

"Are you sure this operation is the right thing to do?"

"Yes." After lengthy discussions with Farrah's parents, I can say this with confidence.

"If that's the way you feel, you have my full support. And you should know I told Stan that even if he thinks it is his OR, it is my hospital, and he will do whatever case you or any other surgeon tells him to do."

"Thank you, sir," I say with relief.

"Good luck tomorrow," Bill chimes in. I am surprised to find him so comfortable with the idea. He has always put the care of injured soldiers first.

"I was worried you might think this wasn't the best use of the combat hospital."

"What can I say, we're both fathers. What more convincing could be needed than that?"

Everything falls into place. With Abe on my side, no one gets in my way. Drew bravely accepts the danger of a round-trip helicopter ride from Tikrit to Balad so he can help give this girl her slim chance of a cure. He arrives safely at our base with his hospital commander, who comes along for the ride.

I linger in the hospital through the night to be sure there are no hitches. We prepare Farrah for the operation with IV catheters and a supply of transfusions matched to her blood type in case her liver bleeds during the operation. I give Stan credit; he comes around and agrees to work with Drew to keep the child sleeping and stable through the long hours of the operation. When 0700 arrives, Farrah's parents give her a good-bye kiss as she receives the sedative and drifts off to sleep. Her father tells me, "We are entrusting her to your hands. Please take care of her as if she was your own daughter."

"Your trust is very important to me. I promise you that she will get my very best." The parents hold each other and try not to cry openly as I take their little girl away from them.

In the OR, we place tubes and lines to monitor her blood pressure and urine output for the duration of the case. On the full-sized operating table, she is a tiny motionless figure, a terrified year-and-a-half-old girl beneath the bright lights that shine on her protuberant belly and deeply jaundiced skin.

When the sterile blue drapes are in place, I make a long incision from left to right under her ribcage. Blood pools up from skin veins that are unusually large due to her congested liver. Her belly is open and her hardened liver protrudes outward like a shark fin, stained deeply green with congested bile. Thoracic surgeon Zack has generously agreed to assist me on this operation, and the very nurses who voiced opposition yesterday are working swiftly and skillfully to keep the room supplied with any instrument I need. I delicately cut away the scarred bile ducts leading to the inlet of her liver. When I see droplets of bile flowing from its cut surface, I create a detour by stitching a tube of intestine to the liver, where the diseased bile duct used to be. Since I have never performed this operation on a child so old, I don't know what to expect. It is a pleasant relief to see that the bile hasn't been completely blocked inside the liver.

The operation goes smoothly. Farrah is double the size of the usual two-month-old getting the operation, and the internal structures are bigger and easier to see. After some delicate work around the base of the liver, Zack and I can safely relax as we stitch the muscles and skin of her belly back together. She is strong through the entire operation. I thank Zack for providing his skillful assistance and we wrap her in bandages and wheel her to the ICU. In a short time, she is breathing on her own and wakes up to gaze into the eyes of her parents, who have waited anxiously for this moment.

It is a relief for us all that the operation has gone off routinely and without a hitch. I have only performed the Kasai about ten times in my life, and never expected to use it in Iraq. As I sip a hot chocolate by her bedside, my surgery professor's words play in my head, "It is better to be lucky than to be good,"

Farrah recovers quickly and is soon sitting up in bed clamoring for food. With each day of improvement, she gradually loses the many tubes and wires attached to her infant body. Soon she is eating table food, and the nurses delight to watch the child with her mother. I can tell they no longer need the assurance of my presence at the bedside. Now that I have tampered with her belly, I must accept ownership of whatever outcome transpires.

Days later I return to the hospital to find Farrah sleeping comfortably in the ICU. Her doting parents, ever by her side, are asleep on a cot. When it is late enough for it to be morning in San Antonio with the time difference, I call home for the first time in days and ask Meredith how she's been.

"Oh, we're fine," she says wearily. "Griff and Reid have a fever. They stayed home from school today." She can tell I am fuming by how quiet I am, and she reassures me that the boys are going to be fine.

We spend the rest of the fifteen-minute call giggling at old jokes, but I can't help feeling guilty for leaving her in the lurch. When I'm seven thousand miles away she is left with sole responsibility of getting the boys up every day and hustling them off to school. Every meal they eat is prepared by her. If one of our boys needs to go to karate and another to swimming lessons, she's the chauffer. It's hard enough chasing after three boys alone, but add the burden of nursing two sick ones, making trips to the doctor—it must be exhausting. I know Meredith can handle it on her own, but I still worry about the kids, especially when they're sick. As the moon traverses the night sky, I feel stretched, my body here and my heart anchored seven thousand miles to the west. I take comfort in a piece of wisdom borrowed from one of my chiefs during residency, "You can't stop the clock." No matter how tough this is, it will come to an inevitable end. I hope Meredith sees some comfort in this, too. Every hour brings me closer to home. Still, yesterday would not be soon enough.

# Sandbags

FOR THE LAST WEEK, we have endured a string of days over one hundred degrees. That is not as hot as it is going to get, not by a far cry. The heat index is only a three on a scale of five. But today, it feels like the sun is closer, like it is touching. The temperature peaks at 117 degrees. When the air is still, it feels like something palpable that parts softly in front of me as I walk. I see heat rising off the gravel, wrinkling my vision. I am not used to heat like this. When I moved my family from Maryland to Texas, the change in heat was a shock, but Iraq is ridiculous.

The recent jump in temperature has hit my plants hard. In addition to the herbs I brought to Iraq myself, I plant a nice variety of seeds sent to me by one of my fraternity brothers. I have transformed the five-foot-high wall of sandbags surrounding my hooch into a near-continuous window box planter simply by stabbing little holes in the fabric with my folding knife and pushing seeds into the dirt. ("Sandbags" is a bit of a misnomer—the nearest beach is 320 miles away, so there isn't much sand here. The deserts of Iraq are to the south and west, near Kuwait. The surface of Balad is made up of a gritty substance you could describe as mud, dirt, or dust, depending on how many days it has been since rainfall. Today, it is dust.) For the last month, these sandbags have served as my own little victory garden. Under my tiny rear window to the north, I grow cilantro and parsley. Shoots of green rise between duct-taped X's that crisscross my little window. Beans and peppers go in by the door facing south. I choose the eastern exposure that gets the full morning sun for tomatoes. Five days ago, at the foot of this wall of sandbags, I started a small row of sunflowers. Shiny tender green shoots are already starting to poke out of the dirt and reach for the sun.

When it was cooler, Sally would come by once every few days to chat. Now that the thermometer has risen she is a fixture out here. She lies on a chaise lounge, sunning herself in the gravel patch between our hooches. The legs of her PTU shorts are folded up to expose muscular thighs, tanned dark brown after a week of regimented sunbathing, and her T-shirt is tied in a knot below her breasts, baring her midriff to the full intensity of the sun. Whenever I pass, she comments on my progress between sips from her bottle of water.

*"Working hard there, Farmer Brown."*

*"When are you going to pour some of that water on me?"*

*"I call dibs on those tomatoes!"*

I didn't know Sally before coming to Iraq, but in a few short months I have grown to depend on her skills as an anesthetist. It is clear that deployment has been a strain on her marriage. She misses her daughter dearly. There is no privacy in the huddled close quarters of the hospital, and I have unwillingly overheard her difficult phone calls home. Separation is like a crucible. It will make a strong marriage stronger, but a weak one will be tested.

On my final trip to the water tank, I pause at Sally's lounge chair to tug a long cool sip of water from my Camelbak. "Just make sure you don't get roasted out here, I think Iraq is a little closer to the sun than home," I joke.

But she isn't listening. There are footsteps approaching across the gravel road. I squint to see the vascular PA Roger crossing the compound with a towel and shower caddy. "Mm, mm, looking pumped up!" she calls out.

"I just got back from lifting. What do you think? Are they battle ready?" Roger does a mock flex, showing off the muscles on his arms. "How are you guys?"

"Much better now that you're here."

He blushes at the attention, chuckles, and continues on to the shower. Sally can have that effect on people. As Roger passes out of sight behind one of the bunkers, Sally turns to me in confidence. "You should know it isn't easy making it through this long, hard drought in the desert."

I smile cordially, but when she clips the brim of my hat, I look past her. As she goes on candidly about the latest tiff with her husband back in Texas, I scan the perimeter where local farmers prop little canopies over young shoots with discarded plastic bags. What appears to be trash, has a deliberate order to it, the straight neat galleries of white bags, a poor man's solution to shield plants from sand flies and the harsh rays of the sun. It stretches my imagination to consider that there

have been farmers, pilgrims, merchants, and soldiers trudg-
ing back and forth over this same dust between the Tigris and
Euphrates Rivers for the past seven thousand years. It makes
our little occupation seem trifling.

Sally realizes I've been wool gathering. "Besides, I tell my
sister when I talk to her."

"Your sister?"

"Come see what she sent me. Being the gardener, you're
going to love it."

With this, she springs up and beckons me over to her hooch.
I follow her up the two steps to her trailer. When I reach out
to open the door, she holds up a hand to stop me. "Where do
you think you're going, fella? You can't come in here: General
Order 1A. This girl obeys the rules to the letter!"

The aluminum door swings shut noisily behind her as she
heads inside. I wait on the steps twiddling the Santa Barbara
and Santa Rafael medals hung on my neck by Meredith before
deployment. Listening to Sally rummage around, I wonder
what purpose I have on this base so far from my family. She
returns to the door proudly holding a tiny blue porcelain
planter with three miniscule cacti.

"That's an appropriate garden for here," I say. "I think
your sister's got the right idea."

As I walk back to my hooch, I decide it is late enough that
Meredith's alarm clock will be waking her up in Texas. After
fishing the emergency satellite phone out of my bug-out bag, I
pop the magnetic antennae for a phone call home.

"It's good to hear your voice," Meredith says, gently. "What
time is it?"

"It's almost three, here. How are the boys? Are they any
better?"

"They slept through the night; they're better. We went
to the hospital yesterday. We couldn't get an appointment

through the nurse's line. They told us to go to the emergency
room, but your friend in pediatrics helped us out. Everyone's
on antibiotics."

"Are you okay? You're not sick are you?"

"I'm fine. Just tired. We're all just hanging out at home
and hibernating for a few days."

"I'm sorry I woke you up so early, I thought you would be
getting up for school."

"Chris, it's Saturday."

The sun must be getting to me. I am so disconnected I
don't even know what day it is. The phone call goes fine after
that—Meredith's handling things perfectly well on her own,
she misses me. But the simple reminder I am no help at home
is enough to put me in a foul mood. By the time I hang up,
I am no longer interested in relaxing back at the hooch. The
only thing I can think to do is run. So with thirty-five pounds
of body armor rattling on my shoulders, I head out toward the
western fence.

There are few others outdoors in the afternoon sun. The
landscape across the runways, to dry farmland beyond, ripples in the heat. Sip by sip I suck over a liter of lukewarm
water from my Camelbak. Off to the east, the smudge of coal-
black smoke rising from the burn pit seems painted across the
hazy sky. Heaps of charred plastic, paper and metal smolder
as they have for weeks in a squalid, mile-long landfill behind
the chain link fence. I know even medical waste from our hospital, including amputated body parts, burns here with the
detritus produced by the 30,000 troops and contractors living
on LSA Anaconda. This close the pit smells like dead skunk
roasting on burning tire. I pass the active center where workers wearing blue particle masks bulldoze reeking garbage into
open pits of flame. I turn north and run through the smoke.
It's only two miles more to the perimeter, but I run swiftly.

By the time I reach the wire I am already out of breath. I jump on the shuttle bus to traverse the exposed eight miles of perimeter opposite the hospital. Dusty rows of plants, hidden from the sun under plastic bags, blur by behind the wire. I get off the bus at the KBR truck depot at the southern end of the base and run three-and-one-half miles back home on more protected roads. We are not required to wear our armor, but I have gotten so used to it I feel naked outside without it.

The mosque on Balad Air Base

When I return to the hooch I am soaked in sweat and feel refreshed. But I don't shower right away. I walk the additional fifty feet to the hospital to water a few more plants at The Swamp, a twenty-by-twenty-foot cement outbuilding leftover from Saddam's regime. I use a rolling mop bucket to pour faintly diesel-scented water into flower boxes set up along the perimeter, listening to the call to prayer from outside the wire as the sun's pink rays cut long and low across the hospital compound. Once the watering is finished, I climb the steps to the top of The Swamp and sit on the roof looking east over the wire across the canals and farms to the palm trees along the Tigris. From the mosque in Bakr Village, the muezzin's voice lilts through the evening air, and the verses of the *adhān* drift over the mile of fields between us. The sun is sinking steadily and the desert air has cooled off. Between the growl of passing Humvees and the chatter of circulating Black Hawks, the cantors' rising and falling tones reach out from loudspeakers of the mosque's tall minaret to call the faithful to the Maghrib evening prayer. I feel naked and exposed without my armor, too visible on the roof, but I linger a few minutes to hear his chant. With patrolling helicopters and Sherpa airplanes to make sure nothing sneaky is going on in the fields, I feel well protected on this isolated island.

# Revelation

DAY AFTER DAY on rounds I visit his bedside. He is a scrawny Iraqi man with sad eyes and a pencil thin moustache. His yellowed skin hangs loose on gaunt cheekbones. Some Marines brought him to us after they found him injured in a field on the outskirts of Balad after a firefight. The nurses tell me that he is one of the biggest whiners on the ward. He cries out to them almost constantly, begging for medication until it knocks him out. When I examine him, he looks up at me and begs plaintively, "Mistah, mistah, morphine!" When I change the dressings on his yellow-skinned belly, he grabs at my hands, interfering with my work. He refuses to do even the simplest task for himself, pestering the nurses through their entire shift to wipe his face, adjust his sheets, fluff his pillows. Still, I feel for this man, a simpleton caught up in this hell. He asks the same worried questions every day but the answers I give do not sink in.

The soldiers who guard our hospital are not quite sure what to make of him. He is a native of Balad, but there is little else they know for certain. Insurgents were killed at the scene of his injury, and it is unclear why he was out in the field that night. One day he is a prisoner with a sentry at the foot of his bed, and the next day they conclude it is a case of mistaken identity and the guard is dropped.

On Thursday I find his bed empty. One of our interpreters, Majid, a soldier with the Iraqi National Guard who works as a part-time interpreter, is leaning against the wall at the entrance to the ward. Majid will disappear for weeks at a time when he is on missions and return to the hospital when he needs a reliable paycheck. Today, wearing his Iraqi uniform and armor, he looks decidedly military. He is taller and sturdier than the other interpreters, built more like an American troop. His chin is shaved, and he wears his moustache close-cropped. His hair is clipped short in a tight crew cut.

"Do you know what happened to the patient who was in this bed?" I ask him.

"That man is gone."

"Gone? What do you mean, gone? Where did he go?"

"He is on the helicopter to Abu Ghraib. You won't see him again, Dr. Coppola." The soldiers behind Majid shake their heads and make a clucking noise at the mention of the infamous prison.

"But I thought we concluded he was a farmer. Do we know for sure who he is?"

"I know who he is. He is a very bad man. My men and I have been hunting for him for a long time. I am glad that your soldiers found him; he has caused us much trouble. He bombed many of our vehicles and killed our men."

I look over at the empty bed, but fail to connect the man who has been lying there the past few weeks to a criminal intent on murder.

"Do you remember the burned girl you cared for until she died, Leila? It is this man who set the house on fire."

I turn to Majid, but say nothing. *Leila. This man killed Leila.* I open my mouth but fail to utter a word. The depth and sharpness of the anger I feel for this man have rendered me speechless. In a moment of vertigo, creased bedsheets swirl in and out of focus, blurring at the edges of vision. Three times I operated on him; my hands wet and warm in the recesses of his belly. I stood over him with a knife in hand, using it to cure him when justice would demand my plunging it into his chest, cutting his aorta, ending his miserable life. Part of me wishes I had.

I retreat to the OR, looking for a sanctuary to collect myself. I slip inside the men's changing area, a muddy corner of the tent curtained off by green surgical sheets, where I find Bill sitting on the bench between stacks of makeshift lockers. He is pulling off blood-soaked boots after another round of gory war surgery.

"What's wrong, brother?"

Blood is coursing through my ears. My eyes blink in and out of focus as the room spins. "That asshole who was gut shot is the bastard who firebombed Leila's house."

Bill stares down at the hollows inside his boots. "Abe told me. I'm sorry, Chris." He stands and lays a hand on my shoulder. "What can I say, that guy was a scumbag. He'll be getting what he deserves in Abu Ghraib. Frankly, I'm surprised we don't have more insurgents in here we don't know about...I half expect any of these Iraqi patients to jump up and try to attack someone."

"When Majid told me they hauled him off, I felt bad for the guy."

"Look, every single time that jerk looks down at the souvenir you gave him on his belly, he'll be thinking of American bullets and American steel."

During my career I've operated on some despicable human beings. I've taken care of a drunk who plowed into a family of five on the highway and lay gibbering in bed beside the parents of the children he killed. I've operated on a carjacker who mowed down children on a reckless joyride before injuring bystanders in a shootout with police. But, in all that time, nothing has been as difficult as this. I am thankful I did not know who the man was while he was under my care.

There is no solace or redemption anywhere in the sad events surrounding Leila's death, so I look to occupy myself with the concerns of the living. I check up on baby Farrah and another young girl with a facial tumor, pleased to find them recovering quickly.

But a few days later I learn Leila's father, Captain Abbas of the Iraqi National Guard local Balad division, was killed in action during a gun battle with insurgents.

# Dear Meredith

April 24, 2005

Dear Meredith,

I started this letter a few nights ago, but I only got two lines down before I was rudely interrupted. I don't like to talk much about alarm reds here, but that night a rocket landed on the compound next to our hooches. Fortunately, there were no casualties. Only one two-foot hole in the wall of an unused building. We all rushed out to take cover in the bunkers. After twenty minutes, the "all-clear" sounded and we swept the area for unexploded ordinances and made sure no one was hurt. When it was over, I was so shaken up I moved my mattress onto the floor to be below the height of the sandbags around my hooch, and fell asleep wearing my armor.

Things have been tense throughout the hospital lately. Since Leila died, I feel haunted every time I take care of a child. It turns out that we ended up saving the life of the man who set her house on fire. I'm glad I didn't know who he was until he was already out of our hands and on his way to jail. It troubles me that the weakest and most defenseless children always seem to get the raw end of the deal in Iraq. Last week we treated a six-year-old girl who was shot in the leg at an insurgent compound. From what I gathered, several insurgents and their families were living on a farm in the town of Qaim, a mile from the western border with Syria. I was on duty in the ER when the girl came in accompanied by US soldiers. As I unwrapped the dressings from her head and her right leg, I asked her to tell interpreter Majid what happened. She told him that the American soldiers came to her family's farm. There were bombs and a fight, and she saw her father fighting with a soldier. She ran over to her father, and the soldier hit her on the head with the metal butt of his rifle. Then the soldier shot both of them. The girl said her father was shot in the chest, and she thought he was dead.

I stopped unwrapping the dressing and blinked at Majid, wondering if I had heard him right. The little girl looked pissed off.

"Is she sure the soldiers who shot her were American?" I asked Majid.

"Yes, I asked her that twice and she says so...but she is a little girl, what does she know?"

Several US soldiers were getting patched up on other gurneys in the ER. One told me they had been watching a group of insurgents planting a bomb. A truck picked up the insurgents and the soldiers followed it back toward the western border. The truck stopped at a farm that seemed to be their base and the troops took it down. The men in the truck opened fire, and our soldiers acted swiftly and forcefully. I asked him what happened to the girl's father.

"I think he's dead."

I looked back at the girl; at six years old she saw no difference between the soldiers and me. She despises all of us. Unless she is in pain she asks for little, but this is not out of fear; this is out of anger. Many of the hospital workers go out of their way to give her a smile, try to make her feel comfortable or bring her a toy, but nothing works. It is pretty awful that she ended up in the middle of a fight between insurgents and troops, but I suppose that's what happens in war.

There has been some good news. The Kurdish refugee boy injured by a land mine went home to his family yesterday. When I learned he was only eating a bite from his meals and saving the rest to bring to his family, I told him I would give him food from our care packages if he would start eating better. I offered him the Oreos you sent me and that seemed to entice him. He left in high spirits, two big plastic bags of goodies slung over his shoulder, and a few pounds heavier.

I also got to work on a beautiful three-year-old girl. When she came to us she was crying and short of breath, with a bulge under her chin the size of two bananas, and her tongue protruding from her mouth. She is a bright little child and disliked me from the start. I'm sure it had something to do with the fact that I had to get an IV catheter into her, and it took several tries to get a needle into one of her tiny veins. Like more and more of the children I see, she came to us by referral. A surgeon at the hospital in Tikrit asked me to travel up there to operate on her, but I needed to get a CT scan first so I asked them to send the girl to us in Balad.

I was able to remove the mass from her neck, but not the tumor from her tongue. It had spread so far that taking it out would have meant removing the entire tongue. It was still a triumph of sorts. She is breathing a lot easier now. I'm trying to stay focused on the immediate goal of getting her through the recovery period, but my mind won't stop wandering to the future. She is going to need radiofrequency ablation treatments to shrink her enlarged tongue. I'm frustrated because I don't know where she will find the proper care once I am gone.

What else? My hair has grown a bit. I haven't been down to the barbershop for a skin shave in quite a while. After a week without a trim, I am in danger of getting kicked out of the baldy club. We, the few, the proud, the bald, posed for a picture with a Bradley fighting vehicle that visited our helipad. Bill was his usual self. He joked that I looked like a senator from Massachusetts posing for a photo-op.

Anyway, I think letting my hair grow is a sign of how much I am yearning to get back to my life with you—the life that doesn't involve Black Hawks laden with IED-wounded. When I get home, I don't even want to go out and do anything; I just want to be with you.

I have to tell you one more story. Yesterday, I was on call during the farewell barbeque, and the helicopters kept landing. Bouncing back and forth between the hospital and the BBQ, I took out two appendices and drained an abscess in a man's backside. The cases weren't all easy. One young man injured in a vehicle crash had a head injury so severe there was nothing we could do to save him. As the party went on outside, we made sure he was comfortable as he quietly died. Three more injured Americans bound for Germany stopped at our hospital on their way from another hospital in Iraq. Two had head injuries severe enough that a neurosurgeon made the trip to Germany with them.

When it was finally over many of the surgeons and a few interpreters met on the roof of The Swamp to take in the night air. It felt good to be up there in the cool darkness after the sun had set, and I could pretend we were sitting together on our back porch in Texas. As dusk fell over the Tigris, we talked about Iraq's future and smoked Romeo y Julieta cigars picked up at the haji mart. Kasim looked at Bill, Brent, and me with the lights of Bakr village behind him.

Our conversation went something like this:

"Whether you stay for one year, or one hundred, it will all come crashing down for the government as soon as your troops go home."

I knew the country was unstable, but the serious look in his eyes made the situation seem even worse than I had imagined. Something must have happened. I asked him why translator Selim didn't show up to work that morning.

Kasim took a puff from his cigar and his shoulders stiffened. "His house was burned down when someone set a bomb off. It is because he works here."

"Is he hurt?"

"No, he and his wife survived. They are in hiding now."

"Who did it?" Bill asked.

"Who does any of these things? It was Ali Baba. He has Iraq by the throat."

"Well, I hope we will see Selim again soon. Is there anything we can do?"

Majid grew furious, the lights of Bakr framing a corona around his American-style crew cut. He extinguished his cigar beneath his boots. "Don't worry, my unit will find the men who did this. We found some vehicles with the washing machine timers used to make the bombs. It won't take long to track down the men who made them."

"I hope you find them soon and teach them they can't mess with our interpreters," Bill said.

"We will. Things are going to get a lot more orderly in Iraq. Attacks like this are desperate. I don't agree with Kasim's view of our country. I think that it would get better a lot faster if more Iraqis would take up the fight instead of letting your troops do all the work."

"Some of us don't have the stomach to be soldiers. Some of us are better for books than for guns."

Majid looked past Kasim as if he were a coward. "This is our country. We have to take it back."

Nobody talked much after that. We all took to the flickering lights of the village below. We savored the last drags of the cigars and quietly descended to our hooches. I imagined this same debate taking place in each of the little houses in the village.

It is good when we can keep a young troop alive so his family can see him again, and I realize I can be useful helping a child who would not otherwise have had a chance. But it just seems like I'm working as fast as I can to mop up a mess that will never be cleaned up. Almost daily, I find myself returning to the same discomfiting thought that we don't belong here: that no matter how long we stay, we can do little to change this malignant part of the world. I know I don't belong here, because the only place I should be is by your side. I dream of kissing you. I want to be home with you and the boys. I love you so much.

Yours, Chris

# Lamb Spine Stew

I'VE BECOME A SQUATTER. My replacement, Jason, has finally arrived, and I was so very happy to see him. He is a private surgeon from Pennsylvania who has been in the Air Force Reserves for the past few years to bring in a little extra money. His usual practice is mostly breast and colon cancer surgery on elderly patients. The work here will be a rush back to his residency, the last time he worked on trauma patients. He seemed a little disoriented, and I recognized that homeless feeling in his eyes, so I promptly surrendered my hooch to allow him to get settled in for his tour of duty. I've moved over to surgeon Brent's hooch, my gear crammed into one corner next to where I fold out a cot each night. Bill and Abe are camped out here, too.

We live like a bunch of bums, all piled up against each other in the small half of a trailer. Days are a goat rope of wake, wash, eat, wait, eat, wait, sleep. We wander the hospital and lounge around the hooch getting in each other's way. The heat outside keeps us indoors, and the available recreation on base lost all charm for us long ago. I tried the pool, but the parade of young, bored soldiers flirting with the few women soldiers preening on chaise lounges in bikinis just made me feel old, out of place, and longing for Meredith all the more.

The trouble is, once our deployment is over, we are spent ammunition. We no longer have anywhere to be and are not of much use to anyone. Soldiers and equipment have to get to the battlefield, injured troops need to be transported out of theater for further care, Special Forces have their mysterious movements on short notice. And in line behind all of them, we wait, and wait, and wait.

The usual routine is to linger around the base until enough troops accumulate to fill a plane. Then a group transport flies everyone to Kuwait, where you wait again for a transatlantic flight via Germany. Bill is working on a plan to get us excused from the group flight plan so that we can make our way directly from Iraq to Germany as space available travelers. Abe insists it's been done before; the trick is to have the First Sergeant remove us from the group manifest and sign authorization papers to fly Space-A.

"But why would he do that for us?" I ask Abe.

"Rumor is he's got a bad flu. I'm sure he'd be willing to talk to a compassionate doctor with a prescription pad."

I am happy to throw my lot in with this little band if it will get me home even one day earlier.

That same afternoon on rounds, I run into Kasim who is translating for the new surgeons in the ER. "Dr. Coppola, we are sad that you will be leaving us soon. Do you know when you will go?"

I answer that question for what seems like the hundredth time that day, "No."

"Well, you must join us for lunch today in our tent. We want to give you some small thanks, and you will be able to taste Iraqi food. Better yet, we will make you Iraqi tea." I can think of little else I would rather do.

According to military protocol, I am forbidden to take meals with local nationals, even translators who work in the hospital. However this rule designed to protect us from food-borne illness has the secondary consequence of insulting the hospitality of Iraqis. In fact, I've learned from commanders patrolling outside the wire that nothing can be learned about the community until they get out of their Humvees and take tea in people's homes. For me, sharing a meal with friends is more important than obeying the letter of the law.

On the way to the interpreter's tent, I stop by my old hooch to pluck some cilantro from my sandbag garden. The sunflowers are doing well and seem even taller than they did a few days ago when I vacated the trailer. I put a few leaves in a Ziploc and head toward the hospital. After a few minutes under the sun I am sweating like a pig.

The interpreters live between the two hospital tents, next to the massive, blaring generators that keep the whole place powered. Their proximity to the center of the hospital campus allows them to respond to the ER or a particular ward at a moment's notice. The instant I push open a plywood door at the end of the hospital corridor the roar of the generators surrounds me, the volume rivaling that of the helipad with several Black Hawks running.

The interpreter's tent is different from the long khaki utilitarian army tents that comprise the building blocks of the hospital. Square in shape and peaked at the corners and center, its earthy red hue has faded to a dusty pink after months of scorching sun. I am half expecting Lawrence of Arabia to push back the flaps and step out in full desert regalia. There is no use knocking or yelling through the din of the machinery, so I reach into the entranceway and part the tent flaps. I poke my head in and shout *marhaba*, using the Arabic for "hello" I have learned from Kasim.

The interior of the tent is a surprising departure from the dun-colored gravel landscape of the hospital's utility tract.

The floors and walls are lined with large Persian carpets like the ones sold in the Iraqi bazaar next to the BX. Some are traditional Middle Eastern patterns; others have a modern touch, sporting prowling tigers or tropical beach scenes. They brighten the space and slightly deaden the noise of the generators. A canopy of multicolored batik tapestries hang from the tent ceiling.

Kasim sits at an office cubicle desk against the western wall of the tent. Every horizontal space on his two-tiered desk is employed with electronics. He has not yet noticed my entrance; wearing jumbo headphones, he is preoccupied with a session of the videogame Halo on one of his two computer monitors. He intermittently tends to the other monitor where Yahoo instant message windows pop up full of Arabic characters. On the top tier, a flat-screen TV is playing a bootlegged DVD of Stephen Chow's *Kung Fu Hustle*, which is still in theaters.

Once he catches me in his purview, Kasim swivels on the seat of his chair to greet me. "Dr. Coppola, I am so happy that you decided to join us."

"When there is a promise of food, I always come."

Majid sits on one of the top bunks, his neatly laced, tan combat boots hanging down. He wears a form-fitting beige Under Armor shirt and khaki cargo pants. "Welcome, Dr. Coppola! You are in for a treat today; we are going to show you what real Iraqi food tastes like."

To my right is Selim. He is standing by a low bookshelf on the east wall of the tent, tending to a thin stew in a dented two-quart aluminum pot. On the far burner, rice steams under the glass lid of a saucepan.

I make a double take, surprised to see him.

"You're back! Are you okay; is your family okay?"

He looks down and smiles modestly. "Yes, thank you Dr. Coppola, we are okay. My wife has sent this food. I know

she will be very happy if you will try it." His voice contains
the graciousness and well-varnished courtesy of many of the
Middle Eastern interpreters I've met.

"Of course, I will be very happy to try it. But what about
you; I heard your house was burned."

"Yes."

"We were very worried about you. Were any of you all
hurt?"

"You are very kind to think of us. None of us was hurt. We
are living with friends and we are safe now. The meal is ready
now. Come, let us eat." His calm is astonishing in light of
what he has endured. As he bows over the stew ladling off the
oily skin, I feel an incredible sympathy for this man, carrying
himself with such dignity, even in the face of misfortune.

We gather around a folding card table in the center of the
tent. Kasim passes out paper plates and utensil packets from
the DFAC. Selim scoops the rice into a Styrofoam take-out
container and places it in the center of the table. He sets the
pot of stew on an Aztec orange trivet. As he stirs, bones, car-
rots, and greens swirl below floating beads of golden oil.

I sniff inside the pot, marveling at the unfamiliar scent.
"Lamb spine stew," Selim says politely.

Majid disconnects the power cord from the carafe and
brings it to the table. In his left hand he clutches four tall,
thin glasses, a finger in each glass. "We made hot Iraqi mint
tea. You are going to love it!"

We settle into mismatched chairs around the table. Kasim
passes bread rolls around. Majid fills the glasses with steaming brown tea. The sweet refreshing scent of mint circulates
on the currents of the air conditioning. Selim scoops a ladle
full of stew onto the edge of the pyramid of rice that faces me.
He carefully fishes out a few of the choice stew bones with
succulent morsels of meat and adds them to the pile in front
of me.

"It smells delicious, your wife must be a very good cook."

"Yes, he is a lucky man to be married," Majid interjects. "That is why he is fat and healthy, and the rest of us are so skinny. Here, I will show you how we do it."

He scoops a ladle full of stew broth and pours it onto the edge of the rice pile. After breaking his bread roll in half, he uses the crust to shovel the glistening rice onto his plate, and scoops a little serving to his mouth.

"It is very good, Selim. Try it, Dr. Coppola, and make sure you get some of the meat."

The taste of home cooking, the tender meat and lightly salted, buttery broth, brings me back to my mother's chicken soup with rice. We all settle to the work of eating, each devouring our own corner of the communal stack of rice, silent but for the insistent rumble of the generator. The interpreters deliberately take only the broth and have nudged the cuts of lamb to my side of the dish. "The lamb is so good, but it is too much for me. Please take some of the meat and help me finish it." After protesting briefly, they all take modest portions. There are many compliments for Selim's family as we reach for second and third helpings.

"Oh, I almost forgot." I pull the Ziploc from my uniform cargo pocket and set the cilantro on the table. The interpreters pass it around, pinching the leaves, sniffing delicately as if I had produced tears of frankincense. They have never heard of cilantro. After attempts to compare it to parsley and basil, we finally settle on a description as a milder cousin of mint. The stew is at the point of perfection, requiring nothing to be added or removed, but they humor me and try a few sprigs on their meal.

The large pyramid of rice soon fades into a small mound. For a full five minutes we slouch in metal folding chairs, so stuffed we are barely able to speak. Finally, Kasim breaks the post-meal food coma. "We will miss you. I hope you will come back to Iraq soon."

Selim quickly adds, "Thank you for the kindness you showed the Iraqi children, and especially for helping my nephew."

It was only a minor operation, but I remember it very clearly. Unfortunately, the day I planned for his surgery we had a MASCAL event and the patient child waited eight hours for a fifteen-minute treatment for rectal prolapse. Despite the inconvenience, Selim's brother was so appreciative he couldn't stop thanking me. Apparently, he told everyone in his hometown that there was an American doctor at the base who could treat children. A week later a Bedouin woman who spoke no English showed up at the gate carrying a four-year-old girl in her arms. She handed the gate guard a torn slip of notebook paper that had only the word "Coppola" written on it. I told them to send her in, and we ended up fixing a hernia the child had suffered her whole life.

I tell Selim honestly that I am just doing my job, but he shakes his head, unconvinced.

"But we know you care. Not everyone does. And I am sure that you miss your family."

"Yes, of course, very much so. I hope you won't be offended when I say I can't wait to get out of here."

Selim laughs.

"I don't want to come back to Iraq with the military."

Kasim smiles. "You don't have to explain to us."

"I want this war to be over, so I can return in a time of peace. As a friend."

"Whatever happens, we will remember you," Majid offers kindly. "No matter what, I think that America and Iraq will be friends. You have done a lot for us."

"I just hope we can make things better."

Kasim raises his mint tea proudly, "Here, here...You've said enough."

We toast to each other's good health and fortune. They each wish me a safe journey home. I ask if they have plans for the future. Majid is eager to continue his work with the Iraqi National Guard. Kasim and Selim hope to stay on as interpreters as long as they can. We exchange e-mail addresses and I depart as the dusk thickens. I can't help but wonder if these men will be alive in a year.

From the translators' tent, I take the long way around the back of the hospital, the sound of the generators reduced to a buzz as I reach the north side of the hospital. I pass the 19th Hole where senior enlisted staff gather to smoke cigars. Departing surgeons have tied the laces of their combat boots together and hung them on hooks twisted into wooden rafters. Near the entrance, Brent's OR boots are covered in brown patches of dried blood. In black Sharpie he has written BLOOD OF IRAQ. On cement bunkers that line the 19th Hole's courtyard, troops have also scrawled their final thoughts. One reads, HAJIS ARE LIKE CIGARS: LIGHT 'EM UP! and right under that one is mine, I CAN'T WAIT TO MAKE LOVE AGAIN, IN A BED, WITH SOMEONE ELSE, AND WITHOUT COMBAT BOOTS. I wander back to Brent's hooch wishing time could speed up.

With nothing else to do, we fight boredom by loitering in the hospital. In the OR, the new team is busy. The recent offensive of the insurgency has made for an unfortunate rush of patients. Before I even scrub in to lend a hand, I see him: the Iraqi policeman on whom I completed my first operation in Balad, four months ago.

He has rallied well and is looking much healthier with a well-groomed beard and bright eyes. He is still too skinny, but is standing on his own two feet, smiling and strong. I can barely reconcile this image with the suffering, attenuated creature that hovered above the abyss for weeks on our ward. As I make my way toward him, my thoughts return to that first call night when medics rushed him into the OR, shot in the belly and bleeding to death, intestines hanging from a silver-dollar-sized hole in his stomach. I was alert, excited, and moving a mile a minute as I identified the source of the bleeding and positioned the tissues for repair. General surgeon Trevor, who was on his way out at the time, was relaxed as we worked together to keep the man alive. Three months and many operations later, we released this man to an uncertain fate in one of the Iraqi hospitals.

When he spots me he shouts across the OR, "Doctor, doctor, morphine!" He laughs at his own joke while the nurses gather around him. They have flocked to clinic to see if this wisecracking funnyman is really the same policeman from months before. For countless hours, they tended to his wounds and administered medications as he slowly crawled to recovery. Now many of the nurses have tears in their eyes.

My mouth must be hanging open; I try to speak but can hardly utter a word. I embrace him, wondering how such a welcome surprise can even be possible.

"How did this happen? How have you gotten so strong?" I ask him. As usual, I have the invaluable help of Kasim to translate.

"It is my mother. Remember you told her that food was my most important medicine? She took you very seriously and is filling me every day."

"Well, you must tell her that I thank her. She has done more good for you than all of us could."

One by one, he turns to each doctor and nurse, speaking with immense gratitude. "I know that I would be dead if it wasn't for you Americans. I want to thank you."

"Have you returned to work?" I ask.

"I'm not strong enough yet, but I'm walking every day. I want to get my job back."

"Your country is very lucky to have a man like you."

We embrace again and I wish him good fortune. I continue seeing patients in clinic and catch up with many of the kids we have treated in the past few weeks. The girl shot in the leg during the raid on the insurgent camp takes her first tentative steps after three operations on her leg. At her bedside, Brent fumbles as he tries to teach her how to load a PEZ dispenser. This is a man I have witnessed delicately rebuild fine blood vessels. The girl's initial sharp glares and skepticism have given way to smiles and giggling.

Later, a teenager whose protuberant umbilical hernia I had recently fixed asks me to take a picture of her with her mother. I see the divide between generations in their faces, clothes, and mannerisms. The girl wears a calm expression, her shiny black hair hanging down to the shoulders of her denim dress. From beneath the folds of her mother's *chador*, dark eyes shine between wrinkles of desert-bronzed skin. Across the years of difference, the broad trusting smile is almost identical. I print out a copy of the photo in the PLX and give it to the mother. Upon glancing at it, she throws up a hand in annoyance that it is not in color. The teenage girl lets out an embarrassed laugh at her mother's bad manners and thanks me.

Today is also my last chance to visit baby Farrah in clinic. She is one month out from the operation to bypass her blocked liver. After surgery she weathered her recovery at home. Back in the hospital she requires a few adjustments in medication to prevent scarring and inflammation from choking off the renewed trickle of bile from her liver. Her blood tests are very promising; the abnormally high level of bilirubin has begun to approach a normal value. At her bedside, her mother has dressed her in a pretty white dress with red ribbons along the hem. Her optimism is contagious, and for a moment I can even fool myself into believing that Farrah looks less yellow today. She bounces and plays in her chair with a happy smile on her face. Her parents, so pleased to have her feeling well, practice the English they have picked up at the hospital. I won't know for months, or even years if the Kasai operation has saved Farrah, but I know that it is working today.

Her father calls me over and pulls a crumpled ball of Arabic newspaper from his pocket. "Farrah's sisters wanted to give you a gift for taking care such good care of her." Wrapped in the paper is a ring stamped with an ornamental pattern of golden rays of sunlight.

"You don't have to give anything to me; I am just doing my job here in the hospital. I should thank you for letting me take care of Farrah. It made me so happy just to meet her and help in her care."

"You must take the ring. It is a very small thing and it is the style of the local Iraqi artists. It will help you remember, after you leave, that you have a family and a daughter here in Iraq."

It worries me that I will not be staying here to see how the ensuing months treat Farrah. I'm grateful that Aussie surgeon Jock has agreed to follow her progress for me. He may not be a pediatric surgeon by trade, but he helped perform the same Kasai procedure on a child years ago when he was a resident, and I trust him.

After leaving the OR for what could be my last time, I wind bored circles around the base that has been my home for four months. Someday, perhaps not right away, I'll miss some things about this place, so I try to capture the novelty of details that now seem commonplace. I bid farewell to my sandbag garden. I visit the flag I fly over the roof of the hospital to commemorate my presence as a man representing the greatest country on earth, even with her faults. I hope the world sees Americans for the hopeful and helpful people we strive to be.

Many suffering individuals have passed through our operating rooms, and we have poured our hearts into our work day after day. And now, in the parlance of the military, it is time to hurry up and wait. We may be spent ammunition, but we leave secure in the knowledge that we hit the mark.

Here I stand at the doorway to OR 1 at the 332nd Air Force Theater Hospital in Balad, January 2007. During periods of heightened threat, we were required to carry our weapon at all times, including during surgery.

# Ro●m for One

WE SPEND FRIDAY the thirteenth of May cramped in the space-available terminal at Balad, watching yet another flight home slip through our fingers as it is converted to medical evacuation. It is well after midnight when we finally hear an encouraging announcement over the speaker. I am so relieved at the prospect of leaving that at first I don't grasp the small caveat at the end of the message. The flight plan has been diverted to Kuwait to pick up HR containers before traveling onto Germany. The airman behind the counter cautiously asks me, "Do you still want the flight?"

The thought of strapping into jump seats beside the honored dead is not what I had in mind. Couple that with the ominous Friday the thirteenth departure, and I think maybe I should stay another day, just to be safe. I am mulling it over when four explosions loud enough to be a controlled detonation on base go off in quick succession. The alarm-red siren indicates an insurgent attack, and we file quickly into the small concrete bunker behind the tent, crouching down three abreast.

It doesn't last. The "all-clear" sounds minutes after we have entered the bunker. Still, the explosions leave us feeling unnerved. When we get back to the terminal there is no longer any debate about traveling with HR.

On our way into Navy Customs, we pass through the amnesty booth where we are directed to throw away any illegal weapons and pornography we might be hoarding. The booth is a six-by-six-foot plywood cubicle soldiers must pass through alone. It is our last moment of confessional before we will be held accountable for every item in our possession. Bill takes the opportunity to yell out, "Coppola, make sure you get rid of all your dirty porn!"

I respond with an equally charming, "You know I sold it all to you, bastard!"

We are giddy to leave Iraq, but the humorless sailors guarding the gate spoil the fun. "No joking in the customs area," one chides sternly. Though I have no donation, I spend my obligatory minute in the booth. On the wall are large glass cases with the most infamous confiscated items. One holds a variety of arms, from small Iraqi pistols up through AK-47s and large RPG launchers. I can't tell if this stuff was being smuggled purposefully, or if some aloof soldier just forgot to unpack the rocket launcher from his duffle.

All the same, I grab my rolling luggage and continue on, presenting my ID and orders to a Navy Custom official who works his way through my trunk, removing layer after layer of clothing and gear. The one item he takes is a river rock I kept from my sandbag garden. "Parasites in the dirt," is the only explanation he gives. I manage to get all my gear packed back in the trunk and head to the plane.

Inside the massive C-17, we buckle into twin rows of rude jump seats that line each side of the plane. The only announcement that we are taking off comes in the form of revving engines and a lurch as we start down the runway. The sandy patch of Iraq disappears quickly beneath us. I shoot a smile to the tobacco-spitting colonel sitting next to me. I have no regrets about leaving Iraq.

We arrive in Kuwait at dawn. It is hot and dry as the ramp opens. We are told little about the airport except that photographs are forbidden. Bill and I head over to the airport bar to sip tepid coffee from a vending machine and watch the Spurs game on TV. Like old friends we are quiet. With little to say to each other, apart from the obvious, we watch the game while we wait the three hours it takes to refuel the plane and straighten out our travel with the Kuwaiti officials.

When we reboard, the cargo is gone. In its place are four rectangular aluminum HR containers, each draped in an American flag. We walk carefully past these fallen soldiers as not to disturb their long sleep, and quietly take our seats. Bright halogen arc lamps protruding from a maze of cables and pipes cast harsh shadows across the deck. Without the cargo pallets between us, we can see each other across the hold. A twelve-foot-high ceiling towers above stout coffins. We exchange no words. The only sound is the noise of the engines. I have seen my share of death these past months, but it was different when there was a chance of saving a patient. Hope was gone for these soldiers before I ever encountered them. Somberly, I think of all the men and women I lost and the many hours they spent flying over the Atlantic in cold, aluminum boxes.

At altitude, the pilot lets us take advantage of the empty space to stretch our legs and walk around the cargo hold. Some sleep; some read books or listen to music. The cargo compartment is over eighty feet long and eighteen feet wide, so we thirty or so travelers have much room to ourselves. With earplugs in to deaden the roar of the engines, we retreat into cocoons of sound isolation. I unroll a blanket on the hard metal grid of the cargo bay floor and lie down with my head on a crumpled towel. On one side of my head are the boots of another resting troop; on the other, I am face to face with one of the flag-draped coffins.

I stare at the box a few inches from my face. The shiny aluminum case looks like a gun or camera case, too cold and sterile for a human, even a dead one. Thin straps secure the flag to the box. The rich red and blue swaths seem much more alive than the box they cover. These men died with that red, white, and blue sewn to their uniforms. All we do while deployed, our every breath up till the last one, is for that flag. Loyalty to that banner makes us put up with rotten accommodations, lousy food, and senseless orders. We follow it without question, some to our deaths.

And yet I have to ask if we've gained anything that equals the value of one of their lives. I think about the reception awaiting me at home and the sad homecoming for these dead soldiers beside me. I count my blessings and say a prayer for their families, whose loss I cannot begin to fathom.

After hours flying with the fallen, it is a relief to feel the landing gear kiss the tarmac. Ramstein Air Base in Germany is greener and somehow more familiar than the desert airbase in Kuwait. We stop in the USO office where volunteer Celeste greets us with a warm smile and a friendly face. Her polyester dress is an older style, big purple flowers on a green background; yet it appears immaculate, with freshly pressed pleats. There is a glittery lacquered American flag pin on the collar of her blouse. After telling us she has survived her husband, a World War II soldier, she asks if we are hungry or thirsty and offers Bill and me a DSN phone to call home from a comfy couch. She may no longer be able to take care of her husband, but we are his brothers-in-arms, and by bestowing a bit of kindness on us, she feels she is honoring his memory.

As much as I enjoy the attention, I am anxious to continue my progress home to Meredith. My colleagues are more relaxed or perhaps just too exhausted to scramble for another flight. When Abe suggests dinner, drinks, and a hotel room, I let him know where I stand.

"I have to keep moving. I would not be able to rest if I thought there was some way to get out of here tonight."

"Guys, I'm staying in Germany tonight," Bill says. "Two days of traveling in the same clothes is my limit. I think a beer and a shower are a better bet than risking sleeping on an airport floor."

Brent decides to join Abe and Bill. He tells me, "I hope you find a flight. And if you do make it home before us, you're not allowed to tell our wives you beat us back."

I tell them to have a few extra beers for me but not to mess around with the St. Paulie Girl. They drag their luggage out into the fading sunlight to flag down a taxi. I am on my own.

There are a few seats available on a Space-A flight departing soon for Dover. The four HR containers are joined by a fifth, all bound for the collection facility in Dover, and the passengers now include a family of five making use of Space-A travel to visit home from their station in Germany. The parents tend to their two toddlers and a baby in an infant carrier. Seeing an American family makes home seem somehow closer. I wonder if we will act differently with each other. I wash down the cookies Celeste gave me with a swig from my water bottle, then sprawl on the deck for a dreamless sleep that carries me across the Atlantic.

On the ground in Delaware, the stars seem to be twinkling at me through a cleaner atmosphere. A bunch of us chip in for an airport shuttle van to get from the military outbuilding to Baltimore Washington International Airport. The shuttle driver is an elderly black man who greets us with a raspy-voiced "Welcome home boys!" as we mount up the vehicle. He leans back to ask each of us where we are from, and I catch a glimpse of the World War II Navy ship name emblazoned across his baseball cap.

My father-in-law is waiting for me at the terminal. As he smiles at me from a distance, his breath forms a mist around his snow-white moustache and beard. We give each other a big hug in the unseasonably cold Mid-Atlantic air. I feel rejuvenated to be with family again but also acutely self-conscious, like when I took my first few steps in the intensive care unit as a medical student.

At my in-laws' house, my boots clomp loudly across their wood floor. I have spent so many happy evenings in this kitchen, but it seems like I am seeing it for the first time. I've taken for granted the warm touches like the canisters of tea and flour, the brightly colored glass in the china cabinet transmitting light in prisms.

"Do you want anything to eat?" my mother-in-law asks me.

"I actually just want to sit still. It's nice to not hear an airplane for a change." Right now this cozy little space is the paradise I have been seeking for months.

"Would you like a beer?"

I almost laugh. "Yes, I would love a beer."

For the next hour, my in-laws pamper me, asking if I am comfortable, warm enough, tired, as I share stories from Iraq. Finally we remember how late it is, and they tuck me into the lighthouse-decorated room my son Ben uses when he visits them. The room used to be Meredith's brother's, and it has not lost its little boy feel. Children's books and toy boats line the shelves of the bookcase, and the walls are adorned with an innocent nautical theme: nets and buoys painted over baby blue ocean waves. I stare up at the decorations and remember putting my son to sleep in this little twin bed on weekends when we visited as a family. Everything seems so clean. The bed has been immaculately made, and the fluffy blue and white comforter is thicker than any bed sheets I have seen in months.

Undressing, I am struck by the recognition of how completely out of place I feel inside this warm and cozy room. Outside the window, I see a clear darkness and the subtle shapes of fir trees. I know there is not a mortar or sandbag around for miles. Even the deep midnight blue tone of the sky seems different, devoid of the threats of the Iraqi sky. Yet I don't want to get into bed, because I fear I will dirty the pristine sheets. I change into fresh underwear, climb into bed, and feel the mattress relax under my weight. After months on a stiff cot, the bed feels foreign. I slide off and stretch out on the shag carpeting. The stiff support of the floor feels strangely more appropriate than the bed. I pull the blanket up to my neck for a few hours rest.

I'm up in the morning before the alarm clock can sound. After a quick shower, I'm back in my uniform and ready to move closer to Meredith. My father-in-law drops me off at BWI Airport, and I board the first flight out to San Antonio. As I walk down the aisle to my seat, strangers greet me and thank me for my service. I smile awkwardly and murmur unintelligible thanks. I do not feel like I have done anything special; in fact my only thoughts are of rushing home.

The rest of the trip is a blur. Eventually we land in San Antonio, and the captain asks for civilian passengers to wait a moment in their seats and allow troops to exit the plane first, like VIPs. As the passengers break into applause, I bound down the aisle and out into the open air of Texas where my bride and the boys are waiting.

Home. What can I say about it other than the indescribable joy I feel to return to family? On first glance, everything appears the same, but walking through the rooms of our house,

I feel like George Bailey, looking through a tunnel into a past life. Meredith and I hold hands as we stroll into the back yard. I shed every last strip of military clothing and take a long, hot shower. It is a true taste of freedom to slip on a pair of shorts and an old blue T-shirt. I stretch out on the couch and the boys bring me papers, pictures, and report cards, catching me up on every missed event. We share a do-nothing day together, all five of us numb with happiness to be together again.

With my jet lag, I get tired at 7 PM and fall asleep next to Meredith as she reads a novel. I hear her quietly shoo the boys out when they try to involve me in a board game. I wake up at 4 AM with my bedclothes covered in sweat, and take a moment to figure out where I am. I've just had an unsettling nightmare in which I make countless abortive attempts to flay skin from children. Meredith's warmth lying next to me brings me back to home.

We slip away for a date to get reacquainted. I try to expunge the few lingering tastes of the DFAC with dinner at a quiet restaurant overlooking the San Antonio Riverwalk. The sky darkens over circling water taxis and dinner boats as our waiter brings us fresh, delicious food, on real ceramic plates. A grapefruit martini and a mojito whet our pallets for appetizers of tempura shrimp over ginger, soy noodles, and mint. We dig into dumplings of ground game meats with peanuts wrapped in crunchy radicchio leaves. I doubt anyone observing us would notice anything more than a couple quietly enjoying a meal and holding hands across the table.

For her part, Meredith already knows nearly everything I experienced while away. Though I may have softened the details or hidden my fear, one reason I have kept my sanity is that I always had her as a confidant for anything I endured. She tells me she is relieved she does not have to be the one to stand up in solitude for the children and protect them now that I can pitch in. I am happy to take that duty again. We talk about the food and share our meals, feeding each other little tastes, but our conversation never dips into serious waters. Left unsaid is the most important sentiment: our relief to once again be in each other's company.

# Coming Home
## May 2005 –
## September 2007

# Reconstitution Time

WEEKEND MORNINGS I walk our little patch of land behind my lawn mower and trim the hedges. At night, fire ants build mounds of dark sand; the ongoing battle with insecticide and seed resumes. Meredith and I sit in the backyard patio enjoying the warm San Antonio spring evenings, sipping beer and sodas, catching fireflies. Nothing has changed, except maybe me.

With two weeks reconstitution time before I report back to work, I upgrade our kitchen and replace the ailing wood in the deck. Having me home is still enough of a novelty that the boys jostle with each other in their rush to help me with household chores. It feels good to be useful to my family again, but I haven't yet grown accustomed to the slow, insular rhythms of American life. I wind my way through the mammoth aisles of Home Depot searching for nine-volt batteries and compact fluorescent bulbs, feeling like a foreigner on strange soil.

Only once have I been to the base since coming back to San Antonio. I had to report to the orderly room within twenty-four hours of returning home. I walked around to eight or so offices, collecting signatures from disinterested airmen shuffling papers and sending e-mails. After turning in my IBA, Kevlar helmet, and gas mask at the readiness warehouse, I didn't know what to do with myself. Returning to civilian life in the States, there are almost too many choices. On every corner there's a different restaurant in which to eat delicious meals. What A Burger. Ghengis Grill. Bill's Barbeque. Biga on the Banks. There are no barbed wire fences; there is no war going on here. On television there is more discussion of the latest American Idol than the troops. Each day a brief tally of the number killed in the war and the latest identifications is buried on the fifth page of the newspaper.

I find myself addicted to any news from Iraq. In the morning paper, I read about a triple bombing at a base in Samarra, and I can visualize the whole thing. (Samarra is an ancient city, holy to Shia Muslims, and home to the Al Askari mosque with its golden dome, and the Great Mosque with its massive eleven-hundred-year-old spiral minaret.) A truck drives up to the square; its generic metal panels on the cargo bay advertising a phony construction company. A bomb goes off, knocking the morning worshipers to their knees. Mothers cover their burned and tattered children and scream in rage. As a group assembles to help the injured, a man rushes in with his robes flapping. He shouts, *"Allahu Akbar! Allahu Akbar!"* throws up his arms and detonates his explosive vest in the thick of the crowd. Minutes later the first Black Hawk descends. I picture the preparations in the Balad ER: the tech positioning litter carriers by the helipad; the OR nurses warming the shipping containers. From seven thousand miles away, I count the wounded and watch them flow through the tent hospital.

It's not like I don't have enough to occupy my thoughts here at home. During my deployment my partner separated from the military, so from here on out I am a solo practitioner, the only pediatric surgeon at Wilford Hall. Pediatric surgery is a limited field to begin with; there are only about nine hundred practicing surgeons in the US and only seven of them are in the military. Fortunately, children are healthy for the most part and don't often need surgical care. Still, the day I visited the hospital to catch up on paperwork, the pediatricians were very happy to see me. The practice has lain dormant for a month, and without a surgeon around, a number of children have been directed to the civilian hospital. It is not because I do so many operations, but for some of the more specialized treatments, it is necessary to have a surgeon in reserve in case something goes wrong. In my absence, premature babies weighing only two pounds went to another hospital where a pediatric surgeon was available to place IVs in their thread-like veins. The military hospital to our north sent newborns with birth defects to the children's hospital in Dallas, rather than to us.

When my reconstitution time is over, I will get the practice going again. In the meantime it is sweet to be a bum, idle with plenty of time to spend with Meredith and the boys. Every time I look at Meredith a stupid grin spreads across my face. She looks at me, smiles back, blushes, and then says "What?" as I continue staring. It is a little Edenic oasis having this idle time together before I start work again. Each day the kids head off to school and we just knock about the house comfortably, content to orbit each other. We don't say much; it is enough just to be close. We go for walks together to drop off the day's mail and return to pick up what the mailman has delivered. Meredith knits a sweater for our nephew as I re-acclimate myself to the living room sofa. If we are reading or watching TV, I reach up and touch her foot or stroke her shoulder, still fascinated that she is just an arm's length away, not leagues across the globe.

One afternoon Meredith shows me an invitation from Ben's teacher to visit his class. "I think it will be good for you to go, and you know that Ben will be so proud to show you off."

It is strange to think anyone would think of my visit as special, but I know Ben will appreciate it. Two days later I arrive at the school and follow the assistant principal across the parking lot to one of the portable buildings set up to handle the rapid influx of new families in San Antonio. As I enter the classroom, Ben grins widely, happy to be the purveyor of today's novelty. It is sort of like show and tell, except I am the curious attraction, the soldier all dressed up. After a round of applause, the kids point and talk excitedly about my uniform and the armor I have brought in. They raise their hands and clamor to ask questions about the darkest horrors of war. I try to be as honest as possible.

A forthright boy with blond hair and clear blue eyes asks me, "Did you kill anyone?"

"No, my job was to be a doctor and help people who were hurt in the war."

"Did you see anyone die?"

"Yes... and it was very sad, but my hospital was able to save a lot of people, even though some did die."

"Were you scared?"

"Sometimes I was very scared, but I knew that I was safe because there were many strong and skillful soldiers protecting our hospital. Mostly I just missed Ben, his brothers, and Ben's mother."

I watch Ben to see if he is surprised or anxious by my answers. He nods with each question as if he would have asked it himself, had we not been so focused on simply being together at home.

"Are you an Aggie or a Longhorn?"

"Actually, I like them both. I'm just happy to be back in America, now, where we are free to pick whichever team we like best. I hope it gets better in Iraq soon, so the children there can start picking their favorite teams rather than worry about their families staying safe in the war."

The kids are most excited when I break out an MRE. Luckily, their teacher Mr. Rector does not mind a little hydrogen gas, so we cook up the MRE together using the water-activated heater. Those brave enough to try the turkey loaf in gravy wrinkle their noses at the taste of the gelatin-bonded chunks of meat-like substance. They agree with me that the imitation M&Ms taste vaguely of soap. By the time I leave the classroom, I have them convinced that the food is the worst trial we faced in Iraq.

After school I go with Ben to fencing class, our usual Wednesday night routine. We attend the Alamo Fencing Academy, a spacious gymnasium housed in a cluster of warehouses out by the airport. Ben's coach, Andrei, is a Russian epee champion. Andrei stands tall and erect, with broad shoulders and the sinewy muscles of a lifelong athlete. A thick scar runs along his right forearm from an injury suffered in the First Chechen War. During practice we often compare notes about our military experience. Andrei's own son serves in the US Navy and will deploy to Afghanistan in the summer. One of the first times we met, I told him I worked at Lackland Air Force Base, and asked if he knew it.

"I know exactly where it is," he said. "When I was in the Russian military we studied satellite photographs of your base."

Andrei is wonderful with the children he trains. With games like Red Light, Green Light and jump rope, he hones their strength, balance, and reaction time without them ever knowing they are working. At the end of class, Andrei rewards the fencers with a practice tournament and commands them to "Dress up!"

When Andrei sees me enter the salle, he bounds across the gym and welcomes me with a big hug. He seems as happy to see me as if his own son were returning home. He stops the class and announces to the children, "Everyone, this is Ben's father. He has just come home from Iraq and I want you all to give him a big welcome back." The fencers smile and give me a warm round of applause. One of Ben's friends gives him the thumbs up. The athletes quickly slip back into a flurry of conditioning and footwork exercises.

I don my fencing uniform, and start warming up with one of Ben's classmates. It might look embarrassing at first, a gangly thirty-seven-year-old fencing with a bunch of ten-year-olds, but I primarily come to work on balance, and am content to be a defenseless target for the kids. While I may never have the speed and skill of one who has fenced since youth, I have taken Andrei's advice to consider fencing "physical chess," and run the match with my mind more than my strength.

I fence epee, right-handed. The epee is a long slender weapon most reminiscent of the rapier, a thrusting instrument used in French and Italian dueling. I use a French grip, my hand protected by a steel, bell-shaped guard. The blade is three feet long with a firm portion near the handle called the forte and a slender flexible tip called the foible. Epee rules are less constrained than those for foil fencing; contact by the tip of the weapon with any part of the opponent's body scores a point. Instead of relying on chalk marks or blood, the modern epee has an electrical switch at the tip that senses a touch. A wire runs up the left sleeve, down my back, and plugs into a scoreboard circuit suspended above the fencing strip by a system of pulleys and reels. Dancing back and forth to attack and defend, we look like marionettes hanging from a string. Meredith watches from the bleachers, proudly cheering us on.

Ben is glad to have me back as target practice. He is all too willing to show off his improved speed. I may have an advantage over him with my increased reach, but he more than makes up for it with the intensity and enthusiasm of youth. I find the only way I can defeat him is to rely on trickery. I draw out his attack and score a point on him when he least expects. That just fuels his attacks all the more. We are both laughing when I deflect his full-speed fleche attack and send him running past me, failing to score.

Ten minutes later I drop my family at home and drive the thirty-two miles to the hospital, to cover the ER for traumas through the night. The next morning I will be helping my friend Tom, one of the orthopedic surgeons with whom I spent so many months in Iraq. He has asked me to help with a teenage girl who has a spine twisted from scoliosis. He is going to straighten the vertebrae of her spine, then fuse them with a steel rod so they stay in line. My job is to open her belly and chest so he can get access to the bones. After he is finished, I will close her up. The long, spiraling incision starts over the hip then curves upward and back, across the ribs, to the spine. I call it the "Poppin' Fresh Dough" incision because it looks like the spiral cut on a pressurized tube of crescent rolls. It is the first time that I'll be operating with Tom since we got back from Iraq. Even though this is a big operation, it should be a lot cleaner and easier than our work over there.

In my office, I eat some leftover lasagna that I have brought from home. *Moonstruck* is playing on TV, one of Meredith's and my favorite movies. I call her up and we watch it together, laughing over the telephone as we point out lines we have heard a hundred times before. After ten minutes, I can hear her trail off, so I say goodnight, fold out the couch in my office, and catch a few hours rest.

At 0730 I make my way to the OR, where Tom is prepping the operation. We take some time getting the patient positioned on a specialized table that supports her hip and shoulders, leaving her spine free to be adjusted. The anesthesiologists place IVs, a breathing tube, arterial lines, and monitors. Once her skin is yellowed with bacteriostatic iodine, I cut a long curve from her ribcage down to her pelvis. Layer by layer I divide skin, fat, and muscles until I have the lungs and intestines pushed forward, and the shiny white bones and discs of the spine exposed. I turn the patient over to Tom and his resident and step out for a rest.

I am extremely tired after having spent the night in the hospital. I never get the same quality rest sleeping in the hospital as I do at home. Perhaps it is the lumpy uncomfortable fold out couch, but it is probably because I always feel on alert when I'm here. I stop in my office for more paper work and end up taking another nap. The hours pass. After fourteen hours of meticulous dissection and adjustment of the girl's spine, Tom finally calls me back to the OR. When we have applied the sutures and put her side back together, the anesthesiologist and I escort the young girl into the pediatric intensive care unit where her every vital sign will be monitored minute by minute.

I peel off my scrubs and change back into my uniform to head home. Just off base I stop at a Taco Bell to order my usual two seven-layer burritos with fire sauce and a 64-ounce Mountain Dew: the bed-wetter. The attendant at the drive-through window is an obese Latina woman, barely out of her teens. Her face hides none of the disinterest in her job. She hands me my order while staring somewhere above me, continuing her conversation through the Bluetooth dongle wedged in her ear. For a moment the two of us are the population of America—a nation of consumers and service industry employees passing plastic to each other. As I drive home from the hospital after dark has fallen, cones of light from arc-lamps on Highway 10 slip over my Jeep like adhesion after adhesion parting in front of me at the shadowy frontiers of my vision. I keep my distance from wild teens recklessly racing through the night in their Japanese motorcycles and supercharged Honda Civics. If they crash, it is not my night to take care of them; I just hope I do not get mixed up in the wreck.

At home I tiptoe through the house, locking doors and turning on the alarm. In the entranceway, I nearly trip over the bag of fencing equipment Ben has dumped haphazardly near the door. I fish through the bag to gather up the parts of his uniform that need washing and toss them in the laundry room basket. The rest I tuck by the door to the garage where no one else will risk a stumble. I am still wired from the operation, so I go into the study to read dispatches from Iraq on the New York *Times* website. I get an e-mail from Farrah's father that reads, "*Al-salam alaekom.* Peace on you, my friend, my peace to your family. Farrah now very good." We exchange pictures. I notice my right hand is trembling when I click the left button on the mouse. The arrow will hardly stay on the file name.

# Adhesions

I AM DEEP into a dream in which I am cutting adhesions. This is a very typical and strangely comfortable dream for me. An adhesion dream is exactly like Tetris fever, if you've ever had it. I think it is common among surgeons.

After a surgery in the belly, or practically anywhere else, such as the chest or a joint, the body heals itself by forming adhesions. In addition to closing holes from needles and incisions, bridges will form between tissues that are not normally connected. Filmy sheets like cellophane join adjacent loops of intestine. Tense cords of scar link the colon to the vagina and bladder. Fat and arteries take shape between the colon and the inside of the abdominal muscles. When a surgeon has to reenter the body after adhesions have formed, it is a delicate, time-consuming grind to separate all of the different organs. It can take hours just to get an open window below the layer of the muscles of the abdominal wall. Move too fast and you end up cutting a hole in the colon and leaking fecal material everywhere.

From the first cut through the skin and fat, I anticipate how dense the previous internal scars will be. Sometimes, if an old scar has grown wide and shiny, I'll make two parallel cuts to excise it in hopes of a better course of healing. As I deepen the cut, approaching the vulnerable intestines, I slow down, separating microns of tissue. Working through adhesions is an exercise in seeing and feeling the border where one organ meets another. Using scissors, scalpel, or the electronic arc of a cauterizing device, I separate two organs while injuring neither. If the fluid that lubricates the intestines wells up in an open cavity between the unscarred organs, I can breathe a sigh of relief.

# "We're not winning, we're not losing"

— George W. Bush

SUMMER LUMBERS ON. The number of US troops killed in Iraq creeps slowly closer to two thousand. After completing an emergency after-hours operation, I drive home in darkness listening to the BBC news report on the radio. Condemnation of the war is vocal in England. There is incredible pressure on Tony Blair to withdraw troops, but he stays solidly behind George Bush. Italy has already begun withdrawing its troops. Tomorrow morning, instinct will lead me to page five of the paper to see the casualty count. By this point I know the cities and rivers of Iraq better than I know the map of Texas.

I receive more e-mails from Ray, the new trauma czar in Balad. He has seen Farrah several times. Unfortunately, her lab tests tell a troubling story. Initially after surgery, the super high levels of bilirubin that yellowed her eyes and skin began to fall. After a few months, levels stabilized at about half of their peak. Yet, on the most recent blood test, they started to rise again. That means the bypass from her liver isn't staying open; internal scarring is starting to form over my operation. While this was a possibility we knew existed, it is an ominous sign for her future. I urge Ray to find Dr. Yusuf, with hopes that he can locate a pediatric gastroenterologist.

Away from Iraq, I feel like I've been taken out of the game. I should not feel this way; nothing has made me happier than the embrace of my wife and sons. At work, it is great to be doing the job I was trained for. But I have hung up my gear when injured troops and children still need me.

Then one morning in August I get an unexpected call from Logan, the neonatologist at Wilford Hall. "Alaska Native Medical Center has a toddler with a bad pneumonia. He's maxed out on the oscillator and he's blown a couple of pneumothoraces."

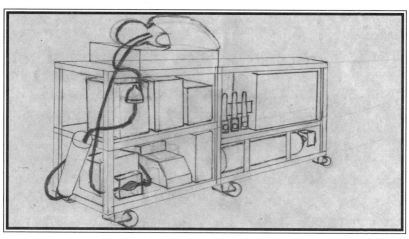

My sketch of the ECMO pediatric life support cart, published in the *Journal of Pediatric Surgery*, March 2007 (Coppola C., Tyree M., Larry K., DiGeronimo R. "A 22-year experience in global transport extracorporeal membrane oxygenation." *Journal of Pediatric Surgery*. 2008; Vol. 43, Issue 1: pgs. 46-52).

Logan runs our Extra-Corporeal Membrane Oxygenation (ECMO) team. ECMO is a form of artificial lung that performs well beyond a ventilator. When the lungs are too damaged to pull in oxygen and release carbon dioxide, the ECMO machine, similar to the apparatus used during open-heart surgery, exchanges these gases outside of the body through the blood. We have the only long-distance transportable ECMO capability in the world. As the lone pediatric surgeon at Wilford Hall, I am the de-facto surgical director of the team.

"When would we leave?" I ask him.

"We are still waiting on Secretary of the AF approval, but we should be flying tonight."

Although the mission is purely medical, the mobilization of resources feels very military. I calculate the distances, hours of flight, and probability that the child can survive until our arrival. We will take a team of twelve people. Because we use military aircraft and crews, it will cost over $100,000. We maintain this capability as part of a promise to military families to provide first-rate care no matter where they are stationed around the world.

As soon as I hang up the phone with Logan, my fingers are tapping out Meredith's cell number. Any sacrifice I make is a sacrifice she makes.

"We got an ECMO mission."

"Where is it?"

"Alaska this time. Sorry, I'm going to have to miss the boys' fencing practice...I know you have a lot of writing to do."

If Meredith is upset, she hides it well. "Well, you know we'd rather have you here, but I'm sure the baby needs you. When are you leaving?"

"The aircrew will be ready in about four hours."

After a quick dinner with Meredith and the boys, I change into a fresh uniform and grab a change of socks, T-shirt and underwear. Meredith packs some snacks and a water bottle for me. With a kiss all around, I'm back out the door.

As hundreds of thousands of San Antonians are slogging through the rush hour drive home, I'm cruising the other way back to the base. I join up with the rest of the team at the hospital and we board an Ambus for Kelly Field where our transport awaits us. The C-5 Galaxy is a massive cargo plane with a 121-foot-long hold capable of carrying two tanks, seven helicopters, or 270 troops. The vast bay absolutely dwarfs our diminutive 1800 pounds of equipment. We ride on the second floor in a windowless cabin, all facing backwards because this position increases survival in a crash. Somewhere over Canada, a warm delicious smell wafts from the galley. I pop my head up like a prairie dog and call back to Jeremy, the respiratory technician, "What's that smell?"

"I'm baking cookies in the plane's convection oven. They'll be ready in a minute. Want some?"

I'll never turn down freshly baked cookies. Munching on warm chocolate chips, I descend to the main cabin and find a small window. Majestically tall pines reach up from the Canadian mountains and valleys, putting the scrubby live oaks of Texas to shame. The sight makes me long for the pine forests of Connecticut where I grew up. Compared to my real home, southern Texas is as much of a desert as central Iraq— years just don't seem to flow naturally without the seasonal change seen in the colors of the fall leaves and the bare branches of winter. I promise myself to return to the Northeast when my time in the military is over.

We arrive at Elmendorf Air Force Base in Anchorage and quickly transport to Alaska Native Medical Center where baby Sean is struggling for life in the intensive care unit. In the nursery, I run my gaze over the tiny patient. Lying still in a drug-induced sleep, Sean's body is swollen from head to toe, a painfully rounded caricature of a little boy. The oscillating ventilator makes the sound of a lawnmower as it vibrates his entire body at a rate of six tiny breaths every second. Four chest tubes over his ribcage drain air and fluid that leak from his tattered lungs. The nurses of the Alaska Native Medical Center provide me with sterile sheets and towels, and

I spread out the collection of scissors, clamps, and forceps I have brought from Texas. The operation I have to perform is simple but delicate. I will slide one tube into Sean's jugular vein to remove blood from his system and another into his carotid artery to return it. It is as straightforward as plugging in two hoses, but his fragile condition and the massive swelling in his neck mean I have no room for mistakes. If I tear the delicate jugular vein, even if he doesn't bleed to death, we will never be able to hook him up to the lifesaving ECMO circuit. With my team gathered around me, and no time to lose, I make an incision in the right side of Sean's neck and sinew by sinew free the two blood vessels from the surrounding tissue. After the two cannulae are in place and triple-secured with silk sutures, I cut into the blood-filled tubing of the ECMO circuit and connect Sean to the artificial lung. Within seconds the color of his face pinks up and the monitor indicates rising oxygen levels. We've traveled three thousand miles, I've worked for twenty minutes, and we are ready to head back home to Texas. We secure Sean to the top of the eight-hundred-pound rolling life support cart. Along with the boy and our equipment we have acquired twenty pounds of Alaskan smoked salmon generously gifted to us by the hospital staff. Not only have I completed a specialized operation, but I feel like I've returned to my proper place, doing what I was trained to do.

As summer turns to fall, the new Iraqi constitution is approved, and I feel like we are witnessing the birth of a new nation. But what a painful labor it is. Every day brings news of more civilian injuries and deaths. No matter what term the press or administration uses, there's no mistaking that this is a civil war. We had the tragedy of one in our country's past and we survived it. I can only hope the same for Iraq.

Before the war, there were approximately 34,000 doctors in Iraq. At the start of April in 2006, the Iraqi Medical Association estimates that 2000 have been killed, 250 have been kidnapped, and another 12,000 have fled the country. In pre-war Iraq, there was already a gross disparity in healthcare available to children depending on their family's social standing. Now things have gotten far worse. I worry about my friend Dr. Yusuf and wonder if he is still alive. From what Ray has told me, there has been no new word from him, a troubling sign given Dr. Yusuf's unfailing devotion to the hospital in Balad.

Farrah's situation is not any better. I hear a discouraging report from her father toward the end of April. Her skin is even more jaundiced, and she itches all the time from the high level of bilirubin in her bloodstream. She continues to have a good appetite, but she hasn't gained any appreciable weight. In the picture her father e-mails, she sits upright in a child's bed made up of pink bed sheets. On a shelf behind her is a collection of dolls, trinkets, and a plastic Snoopy statuette. Farrah smiles with dimpled cheeks. The deep yellow tone of her skin and the sclera of her eyes are more yellow than the Woodstock figurine that stands next to Snoopy.

I urge her father to take her to the children's hospital in Baghdad. It isn't easy, the roads are never safe, and the hospitals are often overwhelmed with trauma victims. He writes me through the awkward translation of a computer, "Thank you for your caring, the violence at every place, caused I can't go to Baghdad to treatment my daughter, so I hope the violence stopped from our life." They live in the town of Ad Dujayl. It is the site of the Shiite Dawa party uprising and unsuccessful assassination attempt of Saddam Hussein in 1982. Saddam responded by killing 148 of the men and boys in the town, torturing hundreds more, and destroying farmlands.

The forty-mile journey to Baghdad is a perilous one, but Farrah's survival may very well depend on it—and that is only the first step. Once her liver shuts down, there won't be any operation capable of fixing it. The only way she can live is to transplant a new liver, untroubled by blockage, into her little body. It seems like an insurmountable challenge. Just before the war started, the medical system in Iraq was reaching the point where doctors in Baghdad's medical city were planning on introducing liver transplantation. There had been successful maintenance of patients with kidney transplants in Iraq for several years. Since the war, the medical infrastructure has become scattered and splintered. The nearest site for transplantation is Amman, Jordan. Farrah's father has been in contact with the Iraqi Health Ministry, attempting to get a compassionate medical visa to leave the country. We haven't discussed details like the money for flights out of Baghdad, or that it will be near impossible for Farrah to return to Iraq if she needs a steady supply of immunosuppressant drugs to keep a transplanted liver alive. One night I receive a desperate, one-line e-mail from Farrah's father that asks, "When are you returning to Balad?"

My uncertain reply is not what he had hoped for. The trip to Jordan never happens and on May 9, 2006, not a full month after I had last heard from the family, I receive the devastating e-mail. Farrah has died. Ray assures me the end was fast, and though I'll never know, I suspect that her struggling liver became cirrhotic, and she died of internal bleeding. I can't help but feel responsible. It was my handiwork inside of her little body that couldn't stand the test of time.

When Meredith and I attend Larry's wedding later that summer, the thought that I have let Farrah down still torments me. But it is so good to share a peaceful stateside event with my friend, and I will not let self-blame prevent me from sharing in the joy of his special day. Larry has come a long way from his divorce. It was his little secret that through e-mails home from Iraq a love blossomed with a friend from church who helped him ease the pain of lost love and war. The marriage takes place in the little chapel in the Villita, the artists' community by the Riverwalk in downtown San Antonio. His bride is beautiful walking down the aisle in a stylish dress. Larry looks different, more jovial. I spot his fancy designer shoes from across the room. This Larry wears a tuxedo and *has* hair, a pale blonde rug whipped up into a peak with mousse like the hero from a forties movie. The two take their vows surrounded by the warm embrace of their family, grown and growing children they have each brought to the union.

Over cocktails at the reception, I talk with Larry for the first time since he left the military. I feel a bit sloppy in my suit, the same one I used for my fellowship interview six years ago. It stays mothballed most of the time because my daily attire is polyester blues or camouflage greens. I'm envious of Larry's stylish haircut. I feel like he is free and I am looking out through the bars.

"You really look great," I tell him plainly as we toast to his bride.

"Thanks. I actually look forward to going to work each day. It feels so good to finally have control over the quality of care I can give my patients."

"I'm so happy for you."

"Don't worry," he says, "your day will come. How much longer do you have?"

"Three more years." Saying it aloud makes it seem like a long way off.

"Do you have a partner now?"

"I've been on my own for over a year."

"At least that means they won't send you back to Iraq."

I want to tell him that I already know they will send me back, but it would be unfair to fish for Larry's pity at his own wedding. We smile at me each other with sympathy and support, but there is a divide between us.

In the far corner of the hall, Meredith and I find solidarity with a couple from South Carolina. For a few minutes we down glasses of pinot noir, dodging the many religious topics of discussion raised by the members of Larry's congregation. When the band strikes up a rock and roll version of "Swinging the Mood," Meredith and I rise to our feet for a turn about the floor. It has been too long since we have danced. Time apart and eight o'clock bedtimes have kept us from a good night out dancing. It feels good to spin her on my arm. Soon we are smiling and laughing, buoyed by memories of other celebrations. The wedding party is full of life and they jump around joyously to refrains of "Twist and Shout." On the dance floor, Larry clasps my hand and wraps his arm around my shoulders. "I wouldn't have made it through without you, brother."

"I feel the same way. Thank you so much for having us."

Larry separated from the military just after we got home from Iraq. His deployment actually ran a month past the date he had expected to become civilian. A stop-loss order was issued. Although it is perfectly legal, it is something the majority of commanders in the military prefer not to use since it means coming in with the heavy hand. To enact a stop-loss, the military has to unilaterally adjust the terms of any agreement they have made with troops. Perhaps in an effort to avoid preferential or punitive treatment, whenever someone is kept in through a stop-loss order, it must apply to everyone in the same specialty. Thankfully, there is only one other pediatric neurosurgeon in the military.

Swearing in as a Second Lieutenant of the United States Air Force Reserve accompanied by my fiancée Meredith Norvell, 1990.

If I did not represent myself transparently from the beginning, let me be perfectly clear now, so that I am not misunderstood. I made my commitment to the military long ago. When I was a college senior at Brown, I needed a way to pay for medical school, so I turned to the military to investigate a scholarship. I discovered that there was actually a financial disadvantage to taking the scholarship. Just three years of the higher salary of a private surgeon and I could pay off medical school debts and top the earnings of a six-year payback as a military doctor. After much thinking, I realized that I wanted to serve for some deeper, non-financial reasons. I had spent my junior year of college studying in Cordoba, Spain. My Spanish friends all owed a year of state-mandated military service. It amazed me that a country with double-digit inflation and a far less advanced infrastructure required citizens to give back to their country, while we in America got so much wealth, education, and protection with hardly any obligation. At Brown, I found myself a minority voice as a financial conservative, deeply inspired by the patriotism that Ronald

Reagan awakened in young people. I had talked enough about it that I decided to put my money where my mouth was: I pledged four years of service in return for financial support during medical school. Later when it came time to train as a pediatric surgeon, I was required to commit an additional two years for this specialized training.

My payback came in 2003 after thirteen long years of medical school, residency, and fellowship. I never cast much thought about whether or not I would go to war, I just knew that we had something special in the United States, and it couldn't continue forever if young people weren't willing to give their support. The first Gulf War came and went. As a medical student I treated some of the troops injured during their convalescence, but I never deployed. In 2003, I began six years of payback at Wilford Hall in San Antonio, the only Air Force hospital that offers pediatric surgery. Meredith and I moved our little family of five to San Antonio and set to work, comfortable to be part of a safe community, steadily employed, with little chance of relocation. Operation Enduring Freedom was smoldering in Afghanistan, and the promise of war in Iraq was looming with the threat of weapons of mass destruction and the doctrine of preemptive war. I didn't know if I would be deployed, but I knew that the Air Force had invested the money to train me for the express purpose of patching up wounded warriors. After our hospital in San Antonio took responsibility to staff the hospital in Balad, it was obvious where I was headed.

Now throughout the summer, the war continues unabated. As I read the paper in the air-conditioned comfort of my newly remodeled kitchen, more than 20,000 troops have been injured in combat in Iraq and Afghanistan. President Bush has just announced the New Way Forward with a surge in troop numbers in Iraq. It is an indisputable fact that as this war continues, more young people will die and more will be injured. They are going to need surgeons in Iraq.

In September of 2006, I present my experience treating children in a war zone at The Trauma Institute of San Antonio conference on the Riverwalk. Although nominally a conference to discuss the regional handling of trauma cases, the many military lecturers quickly transform it into a forum on the developments in the care of wounded troops.

A sad fact is that nothing is better for the rapid advancement of surgical care than the severe and numerous injuries of wartime. With every war, the science of surgery has progressed by leaps and bounds. The Civil War demonstrated how amputation could save lives in the face of devastating tissue destruction caused by the high-velocity Minié ball bullet. In World War I, as the machine gun came into prominence, surgeons realized the importance of aseptic technique and began washing out wounds and debriding dead tissue. World War II brought the revolutionary results of penicillin for wounds infected by the fertile French soil, and prompted public health measures to reduce the lethal effects of malaria in the South Pacific. With Korea came the Mobile Army Surgical Hospitals made famous in Hooker's book *MASH: A Novel About Three Army Doctors*, and helicopter evacuation to aid in the treatment of wounded troops who would have died on the battlefield in previous wars. In Vietnam, surgeons advanced the treatment of orthopedic and vascular injures and developed the capability for effective trauma thoracotomy.

The conference is our chance to spread the knowledge we've gained from treating countless blown-up patients in the tent hospital at Balad. I speak from a podium in the lower level of the convention center. The hallways are teeming with brass: Army, Navy, and Air Force doctors in their Class A dress uniforms, crisp seams on their pants and newly won ribbons from the Global War on Terrorism on their chests. About fifty gather in the meeting room I have been assigned to give my presentation entitled "Not just for Adults: An Experience in Wartime Surgery in Iraq." With a click of the remote, an image of Iraqi children clad in bright purple and orange robes splashes across the wall. They are smiling boys and girls with optimism in their eyes. Behind them is an American Humvee, where a soldier stands in the steel-guarded gun turret, manning the .50 caliber machine gun and scanning the horizon for any threat.

"As you can see from this photograph, the children in Iraq are living, playing, and walking to school on the same streets in which our troops are searching for insurgents who would seek to do them harm. These children, and essentially all civilians across Iraq, are constantly vulnerable to random and devastating violence. War used to be conducted between two armies squaring off, rank and file, in a desolated field or in networks of trenches. Today, war happens street-to-street and door-to-door in areas of dense urban population. Civilians, including children, are far more likely to be victims of war than the military combatants themselves. We also discovered that in Iraq the medical infrastructure was crippled by the chaos and looting that followed the invasion, so these injured and ill children were very likely to show up on our doorstep."

After my introduction and a few more slides, I tell the audience it is no surprise that children suffer a higher probability of head injury than adults. They have proportionately bigger heads, their heads are closer to the ground, and their smaller arms are less likely to be hit by flying shrapnel. I describe how Larry was able to keep children alive, even with fragments penetrating their skulls. That is a surprising result to most stateside doctors given how often gunshot wounds to the head prove fatal here, but in Balad the transport of Black Hawk helicopters was so rapid we were able to rush children to the hospital before the onset of lethal brain swelling. I do not gloss over the harsh realities. I express to the audience how shocked I was when we lost children with 50 percent burns, like Leila. That degree of burn is almost always survivable in a US pediatric burn center. Many in the crowd nod as they recall their own experiences.

Although the staff in Balad did an incredible job improvising, I describe how our hospital was sorely underprepared to care for these injured children. The small stock of child-sized endotracheal tubes and IV catheters was quickly depleted, sometimes on multiple IV attempts for just one child. To restock we often had to use back channels and ask favors of the Critical Care Air Transport teams flying back and forth from Germany. Because our pharmacy didn't have pediatric dosages of some medicines, we had to carefully portion out doses from larger ampoules and higher concentrations designed for adults. Even more vexing was that our hospital lacked an assigned slot for a pediatric expert to intelligently guide the care of children.

"This is not for want of pediatric specialists deployed to the area of responsibility," I say. "Halfway through my deployment, I discovered that the company surgeon assigned to a helicopter unit just a short distance from the hospital was a pediatrician back home. Once I knew she was there, I was able to invite her to round with us each week to make sure the children were all getting what they needed. We shouldn't be dependent upon pilfered equipment and the random chance that one of the pediatricians in country is in the neighborhood. This adds stress on doctors and nurses who are not accustomed to caring for children every day in their home practice. We must properly prepare combat support hospitals to give children the best care possible."

As I pause to take a sip of water and clear my throat, there is some consternation and murmuring among the attendants. One colonel stands up and says, "Are you suggesting that we assign a pediatrician to the hospital?"

"Yes, absolutely. As the slides have shown, the characteristics of modern combat practically guarantee that combat support hospitals will see injured children and likely children seeking care of non-traumatic conditions."

"But the purpose of the medical corps is to treat injured troops," he says forcefully. "We can't go expanding the mission."

"Unfortunately, there is no option. We found that injured children often arrived in the same helicopters carrying injured troops. The mission may not have been designed to include them, but we experienced mission creep."

Another doctor stands up, "If I may, you have to remember what Lawrence of Arabia said, 'It is better to have the Arab do something imperfectly than do it for him perfectly.' We have to allow the Iraqi hospitals to develop."

I have heard this argument before. "I agree the Iraqi healthcare infrastructure needs to be developed. But it was wiped out in the looting that occurred after Saddam's government was neutralized. They haven't recovered yet. We found that the domestic hospitals were barely able to handle routine medical care. Electricity is only available a few hours a day. No running water, shortages in critical items like bandages— I couldn't operate under those conditions."

"But if you assign a pediatrician to the hospital, the Iraqis will start bringing their children to the hospital and expect medical care. We can't have that."

"The children are already there. They have been coming to the hospital from the start. Most of the children who come to the base were brought by an Army or Marine squad who found them traveling through the surrounding cities. Our troops have families of their own, and it is not in their nature to say no to a child in need. Plus, it makes a difference in the battle to win hearts and minds. Soldiers and Marines have told me personally that they have received important Intel leading to the capture of insurgents as a direct result of our hospital's work helping sick or injured children. Refusing to strategically prepare the hospital for children is only hurting the dedicated hospital staff who will treat these children, whether or not we prepare them. I'll tell you it is a lot harder on them if we do not."

The conference is good for me. It forces me to test my convictions before a skeptical audience. By November when Meredith and I get invited to the opening of the Center for the Intrepid, I am beginning to feel more comfortable in my obligation to service. I am not happy to be going back to Iraq, but I've reached a sort of provisional armistice, accepting the duty as an opportunity to care for children who would otherwise be left to the whims of a beleaguered health care system.

On a crisp January afternoon, we arrive at the Center for the Intrepid, a 65,000-square-foot facility with the most state-of-the-art equipment for the rehabilitation of amputees and other wounded veterans. Built with $50 million in privately donated money, including six-figure-plus donations from celebrities like Rosie O'Donnell; Don Imus; and Denzel Washington; as well as pennies given by school children across the nation, the center is an inspiring glimpse into the future of medical technology. The ceremony is attended by luminaries like Chairman of the Joint Chiefs of Staff Peter Pace and Senators Hillary Clinton and John McCain. There is a performance by John Mellencamp, but the true stars of the day are a cadre of injured troops from all branches of the military who gather in front of the podium. Some are in wheelchairs and others take their own steps on newly crafted artificial limbs. Those still in the early phase of their treatment wear hospital gowns, bandages, and layers of blankets to protect them against the chill winter wind. Many of the spouses and lovers proudly waving to servicemen seem barely out of high school. A few are holding bundled babies.

We walk through a spacious two-story gymnasium with a climbing wall and an elevated indoor track that wraps around the dome of a three hundred degree projection theater. On the first floor, long two-track variable-speed treadmills with parallel bars and infrared tracking cameras allow ampu-tees to practice walking on computerized artificial limbs as complicated algorithms assess limb function and balance. Upstairs is a prosthetic lab that uses a computer-aided lathe and three-dimensional mapping to custom fit artificial limbs to the infinite variations in individual body measurements and amputation stump characteristics. One of the most im-pressive tools, the firing range simulator, is equipped with a projection screen and electronic weapon controllers designed to match actual weapon weight and kickback characteristics in order to retrain soldiers to shoot effectively after suffering upper-limb or head injuries.

It is on our tour of the lap-pool, impressive in its own right, that I see a young man climbing into a kayak. He is fit and muscular, apparently in his mid-twenties, with his hair neatly trimmed in a reddish-blond flattop. Both of his legs end at the mid-thigh, and the stumps bear the smooth-healed scars of an above-the-knee amputation. His body works flu-idly. Powerful arms lift his torso from the brim of the pool. He extends forward the tips of his stumps, flexing at the hips, as he swings out over the water and lowers himself into the cockpit. Once he has wiggled aboard, he zips across the pool with deft strokes of the oar. At the opposite end, he dips the kayak sideways to submerge his upper body. Half a second later he pops back out, righting the watercraft with a flip of the paddle. With his lower body hidden beneath the kayak, it is difficult to believe he has any physical deficit at all.

As I watch him move lithely through the water, I wonder if he is one of the men that I treated in Balad. His wounds seem old enough that he could have come through the hospital during my stint in 2005. So many young injured troops came through so fast and were out the door and on a flight to Germany just as quickly as their operations were completed. I strain to remember any of them individually.

In January of 2007 I am put on alert for possible assignment, but a reservist who has never deployed is sent instead. In May, I am assigned to Baghdad. Bill is there, and he e-mails us that he is miserable. He is serving at a small hospital at Baghdad International Airport with an orthopedic surgeon; the only two surgeons on site. Most of his consultations are for hemorrhoids or sexually transmitted diseases. He spends more time sweeping the operating room than he does operating in it. Any of the significantly injured trauma victims overfly his station and are transported directly to Ibn Sina Hospital in Baghdad or the Air Force Theater Hospital in Balad. I'm sure that the inactivity is killing him. We petition our commanders and successfully have the rotation dropped. I receive my hard tasking to return to Balad in September of 2007.

# Training

"It is impossible to love and to part." – Italian proverb

MY SECOND DEPLOYMENT to Iraq approaches faster than I would prefer. I've spent the past two weeks going to offices, supply depots, training sites. Trying to keep my eyes open as I sit in military training classrooms with other surgeons listening to tips about preparing our wills and obtaining free babysitting and oil changes for our spouses. It troubles me that I have to put my practice on hold and cancel clinics and operations for these monotonous briefings, but that's how it goes. A few nights ago I learned I have to go back to MURT (Medical Unit Readiness Training), meaning I must turn off my pager and mind to play soldier on the field site in the brush behind the hospital.

During deployment I carry an M-9, not an M-16, but both weapons are tried-and-true equipment for the US military. The M-16 has been in service, through various incarnations, since 1964. Of the approximately eight million produced worldwide, it is estimated that 90 percent are still in service. The Italian made M-9 has been carried by US officers and security personnel since 1986. In trained hands, it can deliver an accurate kill up to fifty meters away. I do not have any desire to carry either. As medical personnel, I am classed as a noncombatant. There would have to be enemy actively storming the hospital for me to be authorized to draw my weapon. And yet I am forced to cancel a clinic to be able to attend M-16 training. I apologize to the families who need to reschedule. The parents take it easily. One mother tells me "We understand, we're Army. We're used to waiting a long time for medical stuff." There is something wrong when they have been trained to believe that.

At the Medina Training Annex, thirty of us gather in the classroom and await the instructor. The room is a collection of long tables and folding chairs. Posters on the wall illustrate the different parts of the weapon and the clearing sequence. A rolling crate of M-16s is parked in the front of the room. Safety goggles and empty clips are stacked on each of the tables.

Our instructor enters and announces, "Good morning, I am your instructor, Jim; if you are not here for the M-16 training you are in the wrong place." Jim is a pudgy civilian with a bushy brown moustache, square glasses, and a .32 revolver in a leather holster at his hip. He commands the young sergeant who accompanies him to take the roll. As our names and rank are called, we each shout out "Here, sir!" One major, a surgeon, is missing from our group. Jim makes a note of it, and then prattles on about the mechanical functions of the M-16.

He disassembles the weapon with an ease that accentuates his ego. Calling out the names methodically, he holds the parts of the gun aloft, barely pausing to inhale as he explains to us how to clear the weapon after a misfire. From his desk he grabs a twisted piece of aluminum, the remains of a destroyed receiver that looks like an antique. "This is what happens when you fire the M-16 without properly clearing a misfire. The pieces of metal that are missing had to be removed from the face of the BMT (basic military trainee) that fired it. Don't let this be you."

The sergeant unlocks the steel crate and issues us rifles, and we march out in two columns to the range behind the classroom where the morning rain has given way to a cool wind. After an airman passes out rounds of 5.56mm ammunition and helps us load our clips, the range director announces over the loudspeaker, "Take a lying prone position and fire one round into each of the four circles." I ease my way into the one-inch-deep puddle of muddy water in stall #13. The water is cold and quickly seeps through my uniform to the skin. I wipe my fingers on my back, before raising the rifle to my right cheek and sighting the target. At the director's command, I squeeze the trigger, shaking as the gun kicks back in concussive fits. Even with earplugs installed, the noise is incredible. We fire rounds from different field positions and run through a series of targets while wearing armor and gas masks.

Days later a journalist from Yale comes to interview me for a piece she is writing about the effect of PTSD on the returning troops. I tell her what I saw in Balad, speaking all too freely about my lack of eagerness to go back to Iraq and my certainty that I will be leaving the military as soon as I have fulfilled my commitment. When the public affairs office at the hospital reads the published article, they tell my commander that he has to counsel me for expressing my opinion. He calls me to his office. My commander and I worked side-by-side taking care of injured troops in Iraq. He says, "Chris, are you aware that word has come down that I have to counsel you for the statements you made to the reporter?"

"Yes, sir, the public affairs office told me when I turned the article into them."

"Well, consider yourself counseled. Now get out of my office so you can get back to taking care of kids."

I must be on a roll, because only a few days later I see an article in a local paper about the surgical work we did for children in Balad. The article gets some attention in the northern suburbs where I live. After dinner one night I receive a phone call in the kitchen and answer absently, still rinsing off forks and loading them in the dishwasher.

A gruff elderly voice asks, "Is this Dr. Coppola?"

"Yes, sir, how can I help you?"

"The Dr. Coppola in the newspaper?"

"Yes, sir, there was just an article about and me in the *Express-News*. Who's calling, please?"

"I wanted to thank you."

"Pardon me?"

"After I read the article, I wanted to thank you. I got hit in '44. It was in the Philippines. A shell exploded near me and just laid me out flat. I couldn't move my legs; I just lay there shouting. A medic pulled me back through the lines. He got shot while he was dragging me. We got separated and I never got his name. I tried to find him but I never got to thank him. Thank you for what you are doing for the soldiers."

"Sir, that is an incredible story. I'm sure the medic that helped you would be happy just to know that you survived. What's your name, sir?"

"That is all, good bye." And with that, he hangs up.

Griffin, who has been in the living room playing Guitar Hero, comes into the kitchen and asks, "How much longer until my birthday?"

I tell him it is one month away.

"Are you going to be here?"

"I'll be in Iraq, but you can have a party with Mom and your brothers. I can call you on the phone."

"You already went to Iraq."

"Griffin, there are lots of boys' and girls' daddies and mommies over there right now. It's my turn to go again. I have to go help soldiers that get hurt so they can come home to their children."

"It's not fair; I want you to come to my birthday party."

"Do you want to have your birthday party early?"

"Can we do that?"

We convince ourselves we can cheat time by celebrating a future event before I go away. As long as I have been a doctor, I feel like I've been cheating my family, trying to squeeze the most out of stolen moments away from the hospital. The hospital is insatiable; no matter how much I give it, it always wants more. For years of my surgical training, I spent every other night in the hospital doing in-house call. Nights off I was so exhausted it was hard to do much with my family besides fall asleep on the couch, fall asleep driving, even fall asleep while eating. There are exactly 168 hours in week, and that is a fact I learned all too precisely working as much as 120 hours per week during those grueling years. Even when I was exhausted, I pushed myself to do anything with my family, sometimes half asleep. Meredith was always willing to do more than her share of the work at home, but she said it always felt better on days when she knew I was coming home, even if it was only for a few hours before heading right back to the hospital.

Yet compared to deployment, those years of residency seem like a cakewalk. As far as Meredith is concerned, it is like a long day in which five o'clock never comes. I know it is going to be hard on all of us while I'm away. So we do a little fuzzy math—even if Griffin's birthday is a month off, he is going to have us all at his party.

It is high comedy watching Griffin and his friends bowl. Most of the bowling balls are launched from about shoulder height and land on the slick wooden lanes with a thud. We parents sit together and talk about the latest traffic patterns, deals at the supermarket, and how quickly the children are growing up. Our friends offer uncomfortable condolences and promise to help Meredith while I am away.

After the party is over and all the guests have left, we pack up gifts and extra cake and head for the minivan. On the highway, my family is quiet. In the rearview mirror, I can see a dab of leftover tomato sauce around Griffin's mouth from the pizza. The usual teasing and pestering of the family drive is absent. Griffin gazes out at the passing cars meditatively, with an adult interiority and distance, like he can see into the future and is already there.

"I'm glad I got to go to your party," I say.

"Does this mean you have to go now?"

"Don't worry about it. I'm only going to be gone for a little while. I want you guys to believe me, I'm going to be fine and you're going to be fine. You'll see, it'll go by quickly, and I'll be back with you all just a little after Christmas. But there is one thing that is very important to me. I need you to be good for your mother and to listen to her. You have to take good care of her while I am away."

All three boys answer, "We will dad."

We spend the rest of the ride home in silence. Meredith reaches over the center console and holds my hand as I drive.

That night I'm reading a medical journal in our study. Meredith and I have bundled the boys off to bed, and she is working on a new blanket for me to take to Iraq. When the phone rings at midnight, I think it is one of the residents calling me to put an IV in a tiny preemie fighting for life. Then I hear snippets of a familiar voice. In Baghdad the clock is just striking 9 AM. It takes a while to place the voice because I haven't heard it in a while.

"Bill is that you? It's hard to hear, there's a sound delay. It's Chris, are you on the satellite phone?"

"Chris, I'm sorry to bug you so late, but I need your help and I didn't know who else to call."

I sit up from where I have been sprawled on the floor. "What is it? Whatever you need, just say the word. Are you okay?"

"It's not me, it's Cody. He's sick and Isabel can't get him in for an appointment. I've been tearing my hair out over here trying to fix this. It pisses me off. I'm trapped over here and you think the least they could do for my family is help my kid when he's sick."

"What's wrong?"

"He's been coughing for three days and he had a fever of 102. Isabel keeps getting the run around from the clinic."

"Are they up now? Can I call them?"

"Yes, I just spoke to her, Cody can't sleep."

"Bill, I'm going to make sure they're okay. I'll call her now. You'll hear back from me soon."

"Thanks, Chris, I'm really sorry to bug you with this. You're a real friend."

"You took good care of me in Iraq."

"You know, Chris, I used to give you a hard time about complaining about deployment so much, but Baghdad was the last straw. I'm counting the days till I'm out." As soon as I hang up with Bill, I dial his home number to speak with Isabelle.

Cody's fever has broken and she has finally gotten him back to bed. We arrange to meet in the office the next morning so I can examine him. I already have a pediatrician coming to help me in clinic, and the two of us can get Cody taken care of. After sending off an e-mail to Bill to urge him not to worry, I join Meredith in bed and appreciate that we are together tonight. I know how Bill feels. It doesn't matter if it is a major illness or a minor annoyance. It is maddening to be far away when your family needs you.

# Second Tour
## September 2007 - January 2008

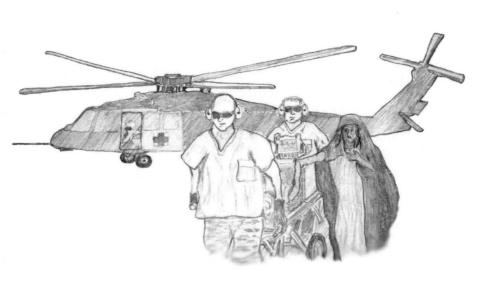

# The Veteran

WHILE PETER GELINAS made his last trip to work in the World Trade Center on September 11, 2001, I was operating on a groin hernia in an eighteen-month-old boy at the Children's National Medical Center in Washington, DC. I was on the second of five patients for the day when the planes hit. When news of the attacks reached us via the CNN Internet news feed on the operating room computer, we immediately cancelled all elective surgery and waited at the ready for any casualties that would come to our hospital. We helped out a few surviving burn patients transported to Washington Hospital Center next door, but our hospital didn't receive a single patient. With the country frozen in horror, I climbed to the roof of the hospital and watched a column of thick white smoke rise into the sky from the damaged west wing of the Pentagon, across the Potomac River, where the hijacked commercial airliner, American Flight 77, had crashed only hours before. It was three hours before I got a call through to Meredith, and another hour still before we located my father-in-law who sometimes works in the Pentagon. And in some strange way that attack is the reason that I am sitting in Qatar waiting for a C-130 to take me back to Iraq.

Peter was my next-door neighbor growing up. When I was four and we moved to Connecticut, we encountered each other exploring the thicket of woods between our homes. With oaks and pines towering around us, toadstools poking out of the pine needles at our feet, I stared down this interloper in shorts and a Steelers jersey standing still in front of me. We immediately staked out our respective territory and became fast friends. Both of us attended Our Lady of Mercy Country Day School and went to Becket in the Berkshires summer camp. Peter was eternally happy and enthusiastic, an avid athlete and natural leader, who by his senior year became quarterback and captain of the Xavier High School football team. Later, he married a beautiful woman and had two boys whom he took camping when they were still very young. His wife was amazed that Peter took a toddler camping and kept thinking they would return home with the tent in tow any minute, but they managed to survive. He worked for Cantor Fitzgerald, an investment banking and bond-trading firm located on the 101st to 105th floors of the World Trade Center. He was only a few floors above the impact zone when the airplane hit.

I wish Peter were still around. In the years before he was killed, we didn't see each other much; but whenever we did, it was like no time had passed. That familiar smile would spread immediately across his face, and he would laugh heartily at the sight of me. We talked about our boys, two of whom share the same first name. It's a silly coincidence, but the kind that leaves an impression.

Six years later it is September 11 again. The base in Qatar looks the same. I am issued my ration card for three alcoholic beverages, but no one is serving this hour of night, and I'm not too interested in a drink anyway. In the giant double-domed shelter, situated in the middle of the base, a scattering of camouflaged soldiers sit at outdoor tables, blending into the furniture. The chow hall is serving breakfast all night. I wash down a steaming helping of biscuits and sausage gravy with four glasses of grapefruit juice. As I leave the dining facility, a stale wind blows through my DCUs and a dull gray dawn lumbers across the horizon. I show no signs of my disaffection outwardly, but privately I am already counting the days. I watch the sun rise until it is time to board the plane and head to Iraq.

In Balad the familiar sights are in their right place, just more built up and established. The streets are the same dusty stretches swimming with Humvees and Nissan Pathfinders. The Sustainer movie theater still plays first-run action movies, but a new protective blast roof is suspended from massive, reinforced-steel girders. The craftsman's bazaar is housed in a brand new warehouse populated with stalls of Greek and Turkish merchants who have purchased base franchises to sell traditional crafts and souvenirs.

Everywhere I look, third country nationals work as contractors. Indians serve food in the four giant dining facilities. Filipinos staff the laundries in each housing area. Turks work in crews pouring cement and erecting walls. Ugandan army troops guard the hospital. There are now 180,000 contractors in Iraq, considerably more than the 155,000 US troops in the country. The word around here is that we have signed a forty-year lease with the Iraqi government for the base. They have poured a deep foundation here; from roots to roof it is clear a lot of money has been spent.

Last time I deployed to Balad, I was a major. I return as a lieutenant colonel. As a senior officer, I rate a "wet trailer," which is a hooch with running water and electricity. I split the trailer with the vice commander of the hospital. We each get half as a living space and share the bathroom in between. It makes a big difference to be able to pee or take a shower without having to cross an acre of gravel at the crack of dawn.

I visit the site of my old hooch, A9. The dirty trailer walls and stacked sandbags make it impossible to distinguish from every other trailer in the vicinity. My herb garden has long since died, and a twelve-foot-tall blast wall has been firmly planted in the dirt where my row of sunflowers used to stretch skyward.

As the base has grown, miles of trailer park have replaced tent housing for most Air Force troops. With separate housing for surgeons and the other hospital staff, social divisions have increased. Doctors sit back after surgery and let the nurses move the patients around rather than help. X-ray techs walk off impatiently if there is a delay rather than pitch in to get a patient undressed. Staff members are more prone to sit at their computer and write indignant e-mails than walk down the hall to discuss a problem in person and find a solution together. Before long, I'm sure they'll be assigning full-time staff here like they do at bases in Europe.

Some of the staff complain that the new hospital doesn't have the same character as the old tent hospital. I tour the new facility with Sal, a trauma surgeon who has been working here for the past four months. I was one of his attending surgeons when he was in residency training. During training he performed a record number of emergency thoracotomies for trauma in the ER. He has always been known as a proactive and aggressive surgeon. That attitude has done well by him in the combat support environment.

As we wander through the modernized four-room suite he stops and points things out, nostalgic for the authenticity he found in the old tent hospital. "In the tents, it felt like an adventure; everyone pitched in like we were at war. Now people just hide behind their desks and write PowerPoint presentations."

When I tell him all the reasons I believe the new hospital can provide better care to patients: that it seems cleaner, that the rolling hospital beds seem a lot sturdier, that it must be easier to keep dirt and silica out of wounds without dust storms blowing it under the tent flaps—he nods his head mechanically.

"That's true, but now that this place is like a hospital back home, people forget they are in the war. When we were all piled on top of each other in the tent people had to deal with each other, so we talked more."

"People don't talk?"

"I'm just glad your team has arrived. I'm past ready to get out of here."

That night the familiar thumping beat of helicopter rotors punctuates the stillness of the wee hours. Shortly after, I hear a hurried scurry of steps on the gravel outside my trailer. There is a loud knock at the door. I answer in my underwear. An Airman in her ABUs with an M-16 slung across her back stands motionless in the dark.

"What is it?"

"Dr. Coppola, they want you in the ER."

"What for?"

"I don't know, they just told me to get you."

My DCUs and desert boots are on in a moment. I ride my mountain bike out of the housing complex, my M-9 pistol thigh rig slapping against my leg with each revolution of the pedals. They have sealed the hospital compound gate across from the surgeons' housing area, so I have to ride around to the entry control point and flash my ID to the drowsy Ugandan sentry.

Thoroughly modernized, the hospital now looks like the other metal buildings around the base. The hive of olive green tents has been abandoned for a network of tall steel and concrete buildings on the opposite side of the helipad. The bare

NATO litters of green canvas have been updated with a retinue of modern hospital beds: padded mattress, electric recline controls, soft cotton sheets. Each patient is given a spacious bay with adequate lighting and a privacy curtain.

On the stretcher in the ER is a badly burnt little boy who looks to be about five years old but is probably at least eight given the malnutrition we see in all these Iraqi children. His face is pink and wet where the blistered skin has peeled away from his cheeks. His reddish-brown hair is caked with dirt and charred leaves. At the side of his bed are two women dressed in *abayas*. One looks to be twenty and the other looks ancient. They stare at the boy silently as he screams and fights with the nurses trying to insert an IV. From the pile of bandages and opened IV wrappers, I know they have been at it for a while without success.

Only a year out of training, one of the new surgeons in our group, Kevin, is pacing around the foot of a stretcher. He is frantic and talking fast. "It was going okay until now. There was one guy shot in the femur that ortho took to the OR. But then this kid showed up. He got burned in a cooking fire and for some reason they brought him here. We've been trying to get an IV for a half hour. I want to give him fluid but we can't get anything. And now there is this other guy who has shrapnel everywhere. He's got some holes in the belly so I think we have to open him up. They just told me that there are two other Black Hawks coming and both have two patients..."

"Wait a minute Kevin, just slow down. We'll split things up and..."

"What are you going to do for this kid? We've tried every vein."

"I'll get an inter-osseous line in his leg. We've got the EZ-IO drill; there's a couple of them around the ER. After that I can get a cut-down. Were you going to intubate him?"

From this close, I can see the tendons clench in the side of Kevin's neck. With some frustration he says, "I don't know, he has some facial burns, but he seems to be breathing okay. I figured I'd watch him a while."

"The trouble is you can't guarantee you will have a free moment all night to check on him. Better to intubate him now."

"Do we send him to a burn center? I haven't done a detailed calculation, but it seems like he has almost 70 percent burns."

"We are the burn center in Iraq. Here's the tough part: he doesn't have much a chance of making it. Most of the Iraqis with more than 50 percent burn we can't keep alive."

By the time we get the boy intubated, the other Black Hawks have dropped off a payload of Iraqi policemen riddled with bullets from an Al Qaeda ambush on their checkpoint. Each of them will need operations on multiple sites; one with a blood-soaked bandage over his neck and spewing a wheezy gurgle of red foam is going to need an operation fast. Jimmy, the trauma czar, has arrived and is calmly directing an ever-expanding flow of patients, techs, nurses, and doctors through the ER. I check in with him to see where he needs me to work. The policeman's eyeball protrudes grotesquely from its socket and blood spurts from his mouth.

"Jimmy, I've got a ten-year-old with 70 percent burns, including facial. Do you want me to take him back or help out with this guy's neck?"

"Go ahead and take the kid," he commands. "Hank's coming in to help operate. With him and Kevin we'll get all these guys covered. How did you get called in, isn't Kevin SOD?"

"I get grabbed anytime there's a kid in the ER."

With that I wheel the boy back to the shiny new suite of operating rooms and begin the laborious process of scrubbing every square inch of charred skin off his body and applying silver, sulfadiazine antibiotic cream and sterile gauze. Hopefully, my prognosis won't come true. Maybe in this new hospital with clean steel walls and spotless linoleum floors we can keep this child alive.

I start by inserting a central line directly into his right jugular vein. I suture it securely to the skin of his neck using shiny black nylon stitches. Now we have a working IV that can handle medications and large volumes of fluid once the IV in the boy's shinbone fails. I direct the circulating nurse to turn the thermostat all the way up. "He's going to lose a lot of heat and blood once he's uncovered and we start scrubbing him down." She cranks the dial to ninety degrees, the air-handling units respond quickly, and we are all soon sweating.

Toiling in the heat is murderous in a full-length surgical gown, but when the heat is protecting an unconscious, uncovered boy missing a layer of skin over most of his body, you learn to adjust fairly quickly. When I worked at the burn center at the Children's National Medical Center in Washington, DC, we would spend full days in ninety-degree heat scrubbing and skin grafting burned children. By the end of an operation I'd drop five-to-eight pounds in water weight. Outside the operating room we kept coolers of ice water to chug between cases. A good percentage of the medical students fainted on their first day on service. On one case, three fainted.

I work from limb to limb, scrubbing the boy's body with a stiff brush dipped in warm iodine soap. Blood oozes from pinpoint capillaries underneath the boy's denuded skin as sheets of skin peel off like soggy beer labels. The bleeding is a good sign because it means that the deeper layers of skin are still alive. But we can't let him bleed too much; this fifty-pound child has only about a half gallon of blood in his entire body. As we finish his arms, we wrap them in dry sterile towels to stem the bleeding and retain heat. Looking at his sleeping face, eyes sealed shut with strips of white silk tape and the endotracheal tube snaking from between his lips, I see Leila. I may have treated thousands of children with burns, but it will be her face I always see.

We finish the boy's legs. Sal kicks open the OR door. He sidesteps into the room to avoid contaminating his out-stretched hands, still dripping water from the scrub sink.

"Hey, Sal, you still here?" I tease him. He's been waiting to get out of Balad for a couple of days now.

"Well, since no one wants to fly me out of this dump, I figured I'd come in and make sure my old professor was doing things right."

"Get your gloves on. We're about to scrub his torso. Two of us can scrub while the other holds him up...What's going on down the hall?"

"Two rooms are running. One guy took fragments to the head and the liver. They had to cric him." He must be refer-ring to the policemen I saw gurgling blood in the ER. Appar-ently, they had to open his airway in a hurry. "Jimmy has your new crew of surgeons operating, so I thought I'd come in here to relax."

"Any word on a flight out?"

"I should be out of here by tomorrow night, and then a week in Qatar." His voice cuts out abruptly and begins again, "Chris, can I tell you something?"

"What is it?"

"I want you to do me a favor. We placed fourteen colosto-mies in children while I was here. Some were babies; some were teenagers. I tried to get them taken down, but our trauma czar's attitude was they were on their own once the emergency was over. He said the hospital was for US casu-alties and Iraqis had to go to Iraqi hospitals for colostomy reversal. They're not going to find anyone on the outside. I've kept a list."

Before he asks I promise to bring the children in for surgery. Exactly how this will happen, I haven't a clue. "You guys must have been busy. Fourteen is a lot of children."

"You don't even know. The strange thing was there were barely any US troops. Toward the end, there weren't too many Iraqi soldiers either."

"Why do you think that is?"

"It's the surge; with more troops we've been seeing a lot less violence. However, there's a side effect." He is looking down at our two scrub brushes lathing the blistered skin off the boy's belly. "Now that Al Qaeda can't get to the troops, they've been targeting civilians. It's frightening."

"How many?"

"It's most of our patients and a third are children."

It is not the news I want to hear. But before Sal leaves I reiterate my commitment to bring the children in for surgery. Fifteen minutes later I am standing in the cafeteria line waiting for coffee when I hear his unforgettable voice. "So Dr. Coppola, you have come back to us."

"Kasim, is that you?" I turn to face a thin Iraqi man grinning at me like a hungry refugee. His moustache is gone and his eyes, which gaze out with suspicion, are rimmed with dark creases. Gone are the dated Western clothes, the acid-washed jeans and Members Only jacket. Now he wears a generic uniform made of the Army-pixilated camouflage fabric, without any insignia. In two years, he has aged a decade.

"I can't believe it's you!" I say, giving him a big embrace, which he returns warmly.

"It is good that you are back, Dr. Coppola, there are many Iraqi children who will need your help. Though I believe that your family must be missing you."

"Kasim, how have you been? Where are the other inter-preters?"

"I am the only one left. All the new interpreters are con-tractors from America. I am the only Iraqi."

"Where are the others?"

"Gone."

I pour two cups of coffee and we sit down at one of the empty cafeteria tables. In an hour the DFAC will be full of hospital personnel, but for now there are only a couple of sol-diers getting a snack while they await transport back to their unit. I have hundreds of questions for Kasim. He stirs his coffee hypnotically with a plastic spoon and stares down at the table as he speaks.

"I have not left this base for over three years now. There is nowhere for me. It has been very hard for me to stay. With each new commander, I have to fight to keep my only remain-ing home. One by one the other interpreters lost their jobs. Do you remember Majid?"

"How is he?"

"Last I heard he was in an Iraqi Security Force unit near the eastern border. I have not heard for him in months. And do you remember Selim, whose wife used to cook for us."

"Of course."

"He took his family to Syria. Everyone I know is leaving the country. I haven't seen my mother in three years."

"Can't you go visit them?"

"Too dangerous. When we come to a checkpoint, we have to guess if the guards are Sunni or Shia. Many Iraqis carry two identification papers: one with a name that sounds Sunni and another that sounds Shiite. Because I am half Kurdish, it will be very hard for me to pass for either. And if I leave the base, I will not be able to get back on. Do you know one summer I lost my housing and had to live in the call rooms? I got no pay for three months—not that I have anything to do with money...finally, a new commander came on and I got a trailer."

I ask him what he is going to do.

"Nothing." He takes a deep breath and collects his thoughts before going on. "Keep working here, long as I can. I work all the nights, because that makes the other interpreters happy and they don't complain about me. I want to leave the country, but it isn't so easy. I need to get a visa, but I can't go to Baghdad safely. If I get a visa I can make it to Syria, but for now I'm stuck. I paid a man one thousand dollars to take my papers to Baghdad, but I haven't seen him for a month now. I don't care so much about the money, but he has my identity papers, and if I have to get new ones, it will be starting all over again."

When I ask him if the Surge is working, he sets his dripping spoon on a napkin as steam rises from the cup. "There is something else happening that is helping more. In English it is called the Sons of Iraq movement, have you heard of it?"

"No, what is it?"

"A lot of the Sunni sheiks are getting tired of the foreign fighters causing so much trouble, so they are helping the Americans. It is partially because Al Qaeda is killing so many people in the small towns, but mostly it is because the Americans are giving them money. These villages are not loyal to the idea of Iraq as a country; they are loyal to their families and the local sheik. The sheik will tell the Americans I can give you one hundred men and he gets pay for one hundred men. The men stay in the same village, but work as policemen, and if they have trouble with Al Qaeda or foreign fighters, they call the Americans and tell them where they are. It is good for the Sunni and bad for Al Qaeda, but since I am Kurd, it will still be dangerous for me..."

With this he leans forward in a conspiratorial pose, his eyes scanning left and right for any eavesdroppers. "…Can I tell you a secret that I have not told anyone else, not even my family?"

"You're not in any sort of trouble, are you?"

"No, Dr. Coppola, I am in love."

"In lo-!" I exclaim in amazement. Then, in a lower voice, "In love? How did this happen?"

"She is in the Air Force, one of your hospital techs. She was here in the spring, Helena, the most wonderful woman I have ever met. She is very different than an Iraqi woman, but I think she is beautiful. I have seen how she takes care of the children here and she is very gentle and caring to them. We started as friends because we worked so many nights together, but both of us knew that it was something more. She has been gone now for six months, but we are e-mailing. There is more to tell; we are secretly engaged. When I can make it to the United States, we are going to get married in her home. She lives in Montana. Do you know it?"

"Montana! That is wonderful news. I am so happy for you." Delighted for him but unsure what to say, I make a perfunctory remark about how hard it must be to live apart.

"That is why I must keep trying to leave Iraq. She thinks that I will be in Syria next month. I haven't told her about the man who took my money."

"You have to tell her, Kasim."

"I cannot tell her. I am too embarrassed. I don't want her to think that I can't handle the arrangements to get out of the country. Or worse, to think that I don't want to come and I'm not really trying."

"The longer you hide it from her, the more upset she will be when she finally finds out. Just tell her and you can work on it."

He pauses for a moment, shaking his head in indecision before announcing, "Perhaps you are right. You may understand American girls better than me. I will think about it."

"I'm not giving you advice because she's American; I'm telling you because I'm married. Trust me, any woman would rather feel like you are including her and she is on your side. I can tell you that Meredith will always be more upset with me if I hide something from her, even if the news is unpleasant. Of course you have to make your own choices."

"I know."

"Is there anything I can do for you?"

"No, Dr. Coppola, thank you. You are very kind, but I will have to solve this myself. Don't worry, things don't happen in Iraq quickly or directly, but if you try hard enough and find the right people, there is a way. Please just keep us in your prayers that we are together soon."

It is a rare happy moment and I feel content as I part with Kasim. I visit the burned boy in the intensive care unit, pleased to read on the bedside chart that he is producing a healthy amount of urine through the catheter in his penis. For the moment, we are giving him enough IV fluid to keep up with all the moisture leaking through his broken skin. His survival is still a long shot, but the chart gives me some hope.

# The Reporter

THE REPORTER ARRIVES unexpectedly late one night. He flies in on a midnight blue sky aboard a Black Hawk helicopter escorting injured troops from the field. When we meet him in the PLX he looks exhausted like he hasn't slept in days. But his voice, measured, convivial, shows no sign of grouchiness. He explains that he is writing a story about the pipeline of medical care from the first contact with field medics back to the United States via Germany. Pulling a pale blue scrub top over a tan striped traveling shirt, he follows Hank and me into the OR with a tape recorder rolling. From room to room, we operate on four of the injured men, washing out wounds and cutting away dead tissue, shrapnel. The Reporter watches intently as we work; for the most part he is quiet but for a few questions about the frequency and nature of these nasty wounds. Two hours later, after the last of the wounded have been treated and are awaiting the flight to Landstuhl, we invite him to the roof of the hospital to get some air.

The three of us sit in a cluster of wrought-iron patio chairs covered in olive green wool army blankets and watch the patrolling helicopters crisscross the no-man's-land between Balad city and the wire surrounding the base. It is 0200 and there is a handful of stars in the sky. I reach for a cigarette offered by the Reporter, and point it toward the roof of the old

Swamp, just next to the wire, to show him where we used to hang out at the tent hospital. The faint, sulfuric scent of the burn pit wafts over us with every gust of wind. With a long drag of his cigarette, the Reporter's unkempt beard glows orange, and he begins to tell Hank and me about his life in Baghdad before the war.

"It was a much different place back then. 2003. Do you know that I was able to live in an apartment with an Iraqi family? It wasn't even in the Green Zone. Nowadays, it would be suicide to live outside the Green Zone. I actually had a little moped I'd ride around the city. I could go wherever I pleased. No escort, no guns, just an American riding around the city talking with the locals. I could eat dinner out in Iraqi restaurants. Families in the neighborhood would make me roast lamb, Iraqi bread, and kibbeh. It is a lot different now. Reporters can't go anywhere without a security escort. Everyone stays in the Green Zone and there isn't the same contact with the people. The whole country has gotten a lot more dangerous. You guys have it good here; such a massive slice of America transported to Iraq."

Hank is sitting upright in his chair, inching ever closer to the Reporter, anxious to get a word in. For now, he lets him continue, "Life is very tenuous here now. I don't even know if the family I lived with is still alive. The Surge may be helping some neighborhoods in Baghdad, but the rest of the country is still unsafe."

Raising the cigarette to his lips, the Reporter relents just long enough for Hank to burst in. "That's for sure. The strategy of this war has been tangled from the start. My brother-in-law is one of the few generals in the Marines so he is at the Pentagon a lot. He tells me it is incredible how much internal strife there has been in the management of this war. A complete and total disconnect between military commanders and civilian leadership, the likes of which we haven't seen since Vietnam. Hopefully Admiral Mullen can do some good; he was here a few weeks ago. Real good guy, personable..."

It's inevitable. During any downtime—in between the hours of frantic operations, after a meal at the DFAC—Hank will invariably delve into political diatribe. But I don't really mind it. Unlike a lot of guys, Hank knows his stuff. I think he has read every book published on this war and countless others about previous wars. He displays the same passion as a surgeon, and his patients fare quite well because of it. He has a very analytical view of the war; it's not so much that he objects to the war on principle, he's just disappointed that so many opportunities to apply the lessons learned in history were lost.

"MRAPs," he continues, "Mine-Resistant, Ambush-Protected Vehicles. They are an incredible improvement over the Humvees. The Humvee has a flat bottom. That's the most vulnerable part of the vehicle! If an IED goes off under the Humvee, the blast comes straight up and can cause devastating injuries to the occupants. The MRAPs have V-bottomed hulls, directing the blast to either side. We've seen MRAPs blown twenty feet in the air, wheels knocked off and engines blown out, but every occupant survived. The difference is unmistakable. Guys in the Humvees had their legs ripped right off, bled to death. Guys in the MRAPs had only minor cuts and scrapes. In fact, the guys in the MRAPs would drive in front of the Humvees because they knew they had a better chance of surviving if they tripped off an IED. I wrote up a memo urging them to get more MRAPs to replace the Humvee. I don't think it's gone too far up the pole."

"You wrote to whom?" the Reporter asks.

"I wrote everyone!" he returns. "I sent it to commanders in field, I tried to get it to the Senate Armed Services Committee. Even asked my brother-in-law to try to get it to staff in the Pentagon."

"What did they say?"

"I got the standard 'Thank you for your concern, we'll get right on it' but there wasn't much change. We are seeing more MRAPs since the Surge, but it's been sluggish."

"The same old 'You go to war with the Army you have, not the Army you might want' that we got out of Rumsfeld," I say. "I know there is a limit to production rate, but look at what happened in World War II. The country had Meatless Mondays and Wheatless Wednesdays to support the troops. Rosie the Riveter was building planes. Look at the citizenry now."

Hank lets out a laugh.

"Seems like most of them pay no mind to the war in their daily lives," I go on. "Have you heard the quote 'the military is at war, America is at the mall'? I understand it may not be pleasant to dwell on a distasteful war, but sometimes it seems like it is only the soldier's widow who mourns his death."

"Where is home for you?" the Reporter asks me suddenly.

"Me? I'm from Connecticut."

"You're East Coast?" He squints and looks at me closely. "I don't see many East Coast troops in Iraq."

"I was actually born near where you live in DC. My dad was a medical student at Georgetown at the time. He trained as an obstetrician down there, as well."

The Reporter squashes his cigarette on the arm of the patio chair. His eyes travel across my face intently, attentive to every word. If I didn't know any better, I would think the tape were still rolling.

"Actually, I lived in DC until I was almost four. We lived on the campus of an all-girls school, Mount Vernon, where my folks were dorm parents. I moved back there again in '90 when I was a medical student at Georgetown for two weeks, but then I moved to Baltimore when I got into Johns Hopkins off the waiting list. I had an apartment on Q Street. I loved DC. I had this shabby basement apartment with a wonderful rear garden. My roommate and I would sit out on the patio on folding chairs. He would smoke Marlboros with one hand and drink Diet Coke with the other. I visited him later in the year and there was a pile of ash on one side of his chair and a stack of Coke cans on the other. I don't think he had moved. He was a great guy; he taught me how to make pesto. Just throw a little garlic, basil, olive oil, and pignoli in the food processor. I miss it. I just miss the United States in general. This will never be home, no matter how many Taco Bells they build here."

"That's right," Hank says. "We will never make this America. The Middle East has been a land in strife for thousands of years. Always will be. It's ironic that we are sitting in Mesopotamia, the birthplace of civilization, and yet again it's the center of a war. Everyone has had a try here. The Persians, the Egyptians, the Ottomans. Baghdad was once the epicenter of world education and culture. Even the English have been here before. It's their arbitrary national borders that created this country out of sectarian populations."

The Reporter turns to me with a half-puzzled look. "Well, at least you can take some comfort in the security of the base. Did you know that since the war began over a hundred journalists have been killed in Iraq?"

Hank doesn't seem to hear him. "I don't know what we expect to achieve, and that elusive goal has made it hard to formulate a strategy. All one has to do is look to history. Look at the Russians in Afghanistan, they had an incredible advantage in technology, numbers, and firepower, but they had no idea what they were getting into. They wanted to install communism and take out Amin, but after they got drawn into the political crisis, there was no way out. They could control the cities and major arteries but there was no way to patrol the eighty percent of the country outside government control. Out in rural areas, the mujahideen used the same tactics insurgents do here—disrupt the electrical grid, blow up convoys, hide in public places where children live. The CIA trained them for God's sake. That's how we got men like Osama bin Laden ready to wage jihad against the infidels. While we were sending them six million dollars a year, they were learning how to arm car bombs and shoot down Russian planes with Chinese anti-aircraft guns. The Russians became the unwanted protectors. Without a set goal they just kept trying to put down the latest warlord to rise up. Over 14,000 of their men died. Of course, the Afghans lost over a million. And they won."

As Hank and the Reporter talk military history, I try to place my own experience in the tapestry of American warfare. But this place has always felt different than anything I ever studied. I can't stop thinking about the way the Reporter said "slice of America" as if the military had just transplanted some façade over here to shield us from the truth. I am so deep in thought I've lost the thread of the conversation. But Hank and the Reporter are both looking at me for a response. All I can articulate are the changes I have seen at the hospital in Balad since my last deployment.

"I mean, it is ridiculous," at this point I am just thinking aloud, "that each Sunday I am fed leathery steak and rubbery crab legs by third country nationals at the DFAC. Sure, I eat it, but as I eat it I think that someone risked their life trucking this shit across the desert from Kuwait. I feel like the base is less secure because a lot of the menial jobs are done by non-Americans making a tiny wage. What happened to Navy cooks and buck privates slinging hash? It is like they are trying to make us forget that we are in a war zone by providing fancy food and selling DVD players in the PX. Private contractors pay truck drivers $125,000 while the combat troops guarding their convoy make $35,000? Is this a war or a corporation?"

The Reporter says, "It's a shame, but you should be proud. Did you know you guys are getting a higher survival rate than in any other war?"

I did know that. 92%.

"Don't forget that people appreciate that back home." He glances down at his watch. The time for the Reporter to depart has arrived. "I can't believe you lived on Q Street. We were practically neighbors."

He gathers his camera and microphone, says his goodbyes, and heads out to the tarmac to join the injured troops on the flight to Landstuhl.

# Grandma

DAYS ARE LONG, and I've been running on little sleep. I am used to sleeplessness; an insomniac at home, but here it is worse. Even in the privacy of my trailer, I still don't feel like I've gotten away from work. I turn out the light but lie awake on the bunk as my head scrolls through images of burned children and gaping wounds, patients who have lost eyes or limbs. I pace around the trailer in wool socks, snack on Slim Jims or potato sticks from an MRE. When sleep still won't come, I snuggle under the blanket Meredith knit and listen to ABBA's *Super Trouper* on my headphones. I write letters home, hoping my words convince Meredith that I am in no danger. I know I'm not alone in my insomnia; half my friends in the hospital take sleeping pills. It's true good meds would probably ease the suffering, but I refuse to take them. I won't submit; I'm the son of an Italian mother.

When my beeper goes off at 0200 I am wide-awake. I pull on a uniform and stumble outside to find one of the outdoor phones mounted on the concrete bunker.

It's thoracic surgeon Andy calling me from the ER about a child who has just come in. "Chris, can you come check out a CT scan?"

"I couldn't sleep anyway."

I bike into the ER where an eight-year-old boy, Raheem, and his father are waiting for me. Like many of the Iraqi children, he is skin over bones and appears much younger than he is. Earlier in the day, he had been playing on a rooftop stairwell when his brother pushed him over the railing. He fell nearly one story, landing belly first over a short retaining wall. He cried a bit but got up and was able to walk home.

Throughout the afternoon he felt well and seemed to be acting himself. Later, when his family gathered for dinner, he tried to eat some bread but couldn't keep it down. After complaining of belly pain, his father took him to a doctor in the neighborhood who advised getting him to the US base as quickly as possible.

The child is in obvious discomfort. He guards his belly against any touch, his legs drawn in like a spider. When I try to palpate his abdomen, he pushes my hands away and cringes. I thumb through the CT scans; bubbles of air that leaked out of his intestine have gathered in the fat along his spine, and a pool of liquid sloshes around his belly.

After paging Kasim, we meet Raheem's father outside the ER. The man is young, tall, thin, with a sharp thrusting jaw that nearly comes to a point. Throughout my examination he sits silently by his boy's side, calmly stroking his hand. *"Marhaba, ana Coppola; ana duktur."* The man smiles respectfully, and I switch to English, allowing Kasim to translate. "It is good that you brought Raheem to the hospital. He was injured internally when he fell. His intestine has burst and is leaking food, saliva, and bacteria. This is serious because the bacteria can create an infection. I am certain that I must operate on him, and it is urgent that I do it now. I know this is difficult news, but the operation is necessary."

The young man wipes tears from his eyes and says breathlessly, *"Aywa,"* first to Kasim, then to me.

I take his hands in my palms and tell him, "I have three sons. I think of them, and I know how worried you must feel. This could happen to any child anywhere, we can't keep children locked in the home. They have to go out into the world and live. I don't know how this will turn out for your son, but we will hope for the best. We will all do our best to help him."

After getting IV catheters in his arms, we wheel Raheem into the operating room. He quickly falls asleep, and the nurses prepare him for surgery. As soon as Hank and I open his belly, liters of a brown cloudy liquid pour out of the abdominal cavity and onto our boots: digestive juices, saliva, stomach acid, and a solution like lye from his pancreas. The duodenum, a short tube that connects the stomach to the intestine, has burst open. Fortunately there is no hemorrhage, but his intestines and fat are irritated from soaking in the caustic fluid for hours. This is a challenge to treat because the duodenum doesn't heal well. The digestive juices are so strong at this location that they will often cut through any repair that a surgeon makes. We are forced to stitch off the exit of his stomach and create a detour to a location downstream in his intestine. This simple blowout of his intestine requires nearly three hours of surgery. I stare at the ceiling and let out a deep sigh; I have let another twenty-four hours pass without a wink of sleep.

In the intensive care unit, I explain to Raheem's father that this red tube is to feed him, this yellow one is to drain the stomach acid from the duodenum, and this clear one is to catch any contaminated fluid that might leak out. He watches his son and listens to me, showing little emotion.

"How long before he can eat with his mouth? When can he go home?"

"The boy's life is in danger, but you should be hopeful, as I am."

I know if he survives Raheem will live in the hospital for weeks and possibly months, maybe even needing more surgery. I do not know when this boy will eat, but we will be monitoring his body very closely, watching for signs that he is ready for food.

Normally Raheem's case would consume my thoughts, but last night's news has left me with a cold stone in my gut. I'm troubled because my grandmother died. It started as an illness I was too far away to do anything about. A lymphoma stole her ability to walk, and she didn't last long after that. It helps to know that Mom and Dad lived in the same town as Grandma, and two of my brothers were close by. She had family around her. It is a long cord across the Mediterranean and the Atlantic, but it is a bond of family so it is a strong cord. There is simply no gentler way I could have received the news than to have Meredith's sweet voice reassure me that I was loved very much, even as she related such sad tidings.

My grandparents, Elizabeth and Ralph Mirando.

By the way Mom described her, Grandma was so uncomfortable near the end it really was a mercy for her to die. Grandpa's death this past year had a lot to do with the decline of a proud, vital woman strong enough to live into her nineties. They had so many wonderful years together. I remember them bickering and annoying each other over petty grievances: it was always too cold for my grandfather, too hot for my grandmother. She would tell him that he was annoying, and he would tell her they were too old to get a divorce. But in the end, the quarreling was water under the bridge. All they needed in life was each other. When I saw my grandma last, she told me, "I had such a wonderful man in your grandpa, and now I've lost him." She didn't think she would live much longer but I told her she had to live long enough for me to come see her again. I wish I had been able to get there in time.

I share my bad news with friends here at the hospital, trying to get out from underneath its weight. I enter the command section and visit the office of our First Shirt, Chief Master Sergeant Harris. ("The Shirt" or "First Shirt" is the highest-ranking enlisted individual in any unit.) He is a mountain of a man with a voice that can reach the back of the drill pad at full commanding volume. He has been deployed over twenty times, including Special Forces missions in Vietnam. "When I lost my grandfather," he begins in a much softer voice than I have ever heard him use, "I was in Germany. A year later, my grandmother died and I was in Korea. It's part of our job and part of our sacrifice that takes us away from home during important events, but that doesn't make it easy. Rest assured, I know what you're going through is hard. If you would like, I will put in a request for your leave to attend the funeral."

"Yes," I tell him, "I would appreciate that very much."

Later that day my commander, Colonel Ryan Isaacs, pages me to his office, shuts the door, and sits me down. I have been impressed with this man from the first day I landed up on station because he always puts his crew at ease. The only time he intervenes in the hospital is when there is a serious problem. He gets us what we need and staves off interference.

With his fingers interlaced behind a paperweight, he looks into my eyes.

"Tell me about your grandmother."

"They lived just up the Connecticut shore," I begin hesitantly, "in West Haven. We'd go to their house every week. While my grandmother cooked for us, we'd go fishing with my grandfather down at the pier. We never caught much, maybe some snappers and an occasional blue, but it was fun just to be with him. When he talked, his voice held the rhythm of the waves splashing on the pylons below us."

Colonel Isaacs nods as I tell my story.

"Back at the house, Grandma had the whole kitchen going. Most of what I know about cooking I learned from her, and what she didn't teach me I learned from my mother who learned from Grandma. Her meat sauce was incredible. She would add pork ribs, sausage, and braciola, but we would call it 'brazhawl' because that's the dialect in southern Italy. Our family is from Amalfi, a little fishing village south of Naples. Everyone there makes a living from the sea. That's why the Amalfidon settled in New Haven when they crossed the ocean...Her braciola were incredible. She would pound the steak so thin and roll it with layers of Parmigiana cheese and fresh parsley from the garden, then tie it up in twine so it wouldn't fall apart in the sauce. After we ate, she would send us home with so much food that it would last until we saw her again.

"Everything she made was so good, except maybe her fried chicken. She used such tiny chickens and so little oil in the pan they ended up like dry little nuggets rolled in bread crumbs. My dad called it 'punishment chicken' because he must have done something wrong to deserve it. Grandma would swat her hands at my father and exclaim 'Ayyy!' but it would always get her laughing. Sure enough, every week my father and I would finish all the punishment chicken. He was an OB/GYN, with a lot of late nights on call, so we would sometimes share a midnight snack together when he got home. The chicken tasted just fine with a little oil and vinegar."

Colonel Isaacs is grinning, and I am too. "I'm sorry I can't get you home for the funeral, Chris. They are pretty strict that you can only leave for a grandparent's funeral if they raised you in *loco parentis*. But remember that we are each other's family while we are over here. These are good people and you can depend on them."

Throughout the day the generosity and kind words of hospital staff continue to lift my spirits. When Kasim hears my bad news that evening in the DFAC, he immediately gives me a hug and brings me a cup of coffee with hot chocolate mix in it, just how I like it. He agrees with me that grandmothers have a magical way of making you feel like a good person. When his grandmother died he felt terrible that he could not get off the base to go visit his family and pay his respects. It was a full year and a half before the danger subsided and Kasim was able to visit his family. That was the last time he saw his mother.

"I am telling you this," Kasim adds, "because I want you to know that my heart is with your heart. Because I know that you must feel the same sadness to be far from her."

"With all the danger in Iraq, Connecticut seems a whole lot closer than your family," I say candidly. I am grateful for his empathy. He is the oldest friend I have in Balad.

We sit silently for a few minutes, slowly stirring our coffee beneath the fluorescent glow of the hanging DFAC lights. It is a sober, patient silence that reminds me of nights I used to sit here with Larry, struggling with the arbitrary nature of death. After some time I ask, "Have you made any progress on your passport? Has your contact come back to the base?"

"Yes, he came back."

"You don't sound happy about it."

"There was a problem. My name is misspelled in the passport. It doesn't match my other papers. I didn't discover the mistake until I had already given him nearly a thousand dollars."

"He should do it again then."

"He is asking for more money to fix it, and it is like he is laughing at me now. He knows that I cannot leave the base, and he treats me like I have become his open bank account."

"Is the problem money?"

"No, it is not money. I have the money saved up. Every month I get a paycheck, and there is nowhere for me to spend it. The problem is trust. I would pay him ten times as much if I had any confidence he was not a cheat and a liar. But that is my problem. I have to put my fate in the hands of a devil."

When I lie down to bed that night I can't sleep. I keep thinking about Kasim's words, "I have put my fate in the hands of a devil." I am struck by the similarity of our predicaments, both of us isolated from our families and stuck in a war-torn country we cannot wait to leave. But is this something he has chosen? I have chosen? And why is Kasim suddenly so desperate to leave Iraq? Whenever we've spoken in the past he has always been resigned about his time here, never this restless. I know the danger of execution by Al Qaeda is real for Iraqi translators like Kasim—there are few horrors worse than insurgents armed with electric drills—but I imagine his anxiety is not out of fear of harm, but desperation to reunite with a woman he loves. In this, he is not alone.

I return to the hospital eight hours later and immediately check in on Raheem. I notice difficulty with his vital signs. We try medicine to stimulate his heart, but his heart rhythm slows then stops altogether. The nurses and technicians quickly circle and help. One pushes on his chest to keep the blood flowing. After several minutes and different medications, his heart starts to beat.

In a half breath I am at the bedside of Nasir, a fifteen-year-old patient in our midst for about a month now. He was shot in the belly in a marketplace and the bullet ruptured his aorta, the biggest blood vessel in the body. With so much blood running through it, when the aorta gets ruptured most people bleed to death in a few minutes. Those like Nasir lucky enough to survive are called an "incredible save."

The good news is that since his tracheostomy the boy has begun talking again. I have put tubes through the skin of his belly to remove fluid and begun feeding him liquid nutrition similar to baby formula. He is walking and taking sips of liquid. But after nearly ten operations and a month without a good meal, he is skinny as a rail.

Today on rounds, I realize I will have to try something new because he has begun leaking stomach acid out of the hole in his belly. A leaky stomach is a frustrating, bang-your-head-on-the-wall nuisance to solve. The wet environment in a stomach wound makes each day's progress just dissolve and fall away. I have tried creams, bags, catheters, and have even resorted to an additional operation to get these holes closed. Whatever the method, it is never an easy recovery. In someone who is just feathers over bone like this young man, it can even mean death.

In the hospital we have a supply of suction devices like vacuum-packed sponges, which suck fluid from open wounds and make wounds heal faster. In the past, we have put them on legs, arms, genitals, and any of the unlimited variety of places that shrapnel can tear through a body. This morning I rig one to the hole around the nutrition tube in this boy's belly, and it sticks. I was concerned the sponge would suck his stomach empty, but when he drank bottled water for me, none of it leaked. If it works, this may be a new weapon in my arsenal.

When I finish applying the device, his elderly grandmother, who has slept all night by the side of the child's hospital bed, breaks into a long excited statement complete with hand gestures. I look to Kasim, who explains that all she has just said roughly means "thank you" but is embellished with specific requests to Allah to make our lives easier by clearing the obstacles in front of us. I am pleased with the results of the suction sponge. If we have the leak plugged, we can get to work fattening the boy up and making him strong again.

Next door in the ICU, however, the mood is much quieter. Raheem is in a flat spin. Bacteria still leak into his blood. The swelling has worsened, and the blood supply to his kidney is being strangled by pressure from his bloated intestine. He needs his abdomen opened to relieve this pressure.

We do the operation right there in the ICU. He is too sick to be moved. I leave the cut on his belly open with a clear layer of plastic covering his intestines. It will have to stay open until the swelling goes down. Through the day, his legs turn cold and he stops making urine. He receives several strong medications. I'm amazed he is still hanging in there.

I have spoken with his father many times. His English is limited. I have heard him say "good" and "thank you," but neither seems very useful at this time. Raheem is the same age as our middle boy, Griffin. In his father's eyes, I see incredible fear and pain. I don't claim to know the future. I do not conceal from this man my low expectations that his son will live, but as long as he is here we will keep fighting for him. The nurses and technicians in the ICU are working faithfully to keep him alive. We are going to stick by this boy, but if his heart stops again, I have little hope we will get it restarted.

It is not until after midnight that the young father falls asleep in a chair, his shoulders and upper body slouched over the bed at his son's feet. He exhausted himself waiting for a hopeful sign of improvement that never came. I silently check vital signs, careful not to disturb them.

I'm backup SOD for the evening, behind Hank. We've only a few hours until dawn when we will pass the baton. My eyes dim and my head bobs. I feel the need for the night's next dose of coffee lifted from the anesthesiologists' lounge. I hope I make it till morning. I hope Raheem makes it till morning, too.

Two days later I miss my Grandma's funeral. Dear friends write to tell me about the ceremony. My brother Adam read aloud a letter sent on my behalf, and it felt like I was there in some small way. But it is hard to grieve from a distance. I've closed my heart, and I don't think I will be able to open it until I get back home. My relationship with her didn't merit presence at her funeral in the eyes of the military. It's as if they were afraid I was going to run off and dodge my return flight to Iraq. I'm not a child. I despise being treated like a seventeen-year-old recruit.

Through the night I watch Raheem struggle to stay alive in the ICU. One by one his organs start failing. His heart can barely mount enough force to circulate his blood. We pump powerful stimulants into his bloodstream to keep his heart beating. His kidneys have made no urine in days. His immune system weakens, and the remaining white blood cells die off. I increase the pressure of the ventilator, hoping it will force more air in and out of his lungs. I loosen the dressing over his belly to allow more room for his swollen intestine to bulge out. Nothing works. There is a sudden drop in his oxygen level. We have already agreed with his father that we won't push on his chest to restart his heart if it stops. We make a desperate attempt to stave off the inevitable with a volley of drugs and a replacement of his breathing tube. It is all for naught. His heart weakens, slows, and stops for good. Our efforts were well intentioned, but we started too far behind the eight ball. Sepsis is a term that indicates an infection has spread throughout the body. The word basically means contamination, which is an accurate description for what happens when bacteria overwhelm a body's defenses and travel throughout the blood stream. Perhaps if we had chosen different antibiotics or different fluids things might have been different. Who knows?

His father is close to us during the resuscitation attempt. Kasim sits with him while I work. I tell him I have failed and Raheem is dead. It doesn't matter that I have been warning him about this for days. Nothing can prepare a man for this. He wails. He runs to his son's bedside and collapses over the bedrail. He covers his little boy's swollen face in kisses as he sobs his name. I stand beside him, an empty shell, drained of ideas and energy. He looks to me and motions with his hand at Raheem's belly. His eyes implore me as he speaks and I don't need Kasim's interpretation to know that he is asking me to sew his son's belly shut.

I gather some instruments from the operating room. A young technician helps me as I close the incision on Raheem's abdomen. The tech tells me that this is the first time a patient in his care has died. I am sorry that it has to be a child. I remember my first patient to die, thirteen years ago when I was an intern. I remember how damaged I felt after the obese man, convulsing with a massive blood clot in his brain, took his final breath. I don't share this with the young tech. I advise him to look ahead to the next patient and hope for victory. He helps me as I stitch a long seam up the boy's incision. I try hard not to tear his intestines. I have to remind myself that it is too late for that to do any good. I couldn't give him what he needed, but I gave him the little that I could. I squint to focus and my eyes burn as I tie the last knot. The ICU nurse enters to clean Raheem's body before he is sent down the hall to the morgue.

# This Is Why It's Hard

*Nov. 12, 2007*

Despite all the encouragement from friends, Iraq has turned into a dark place since my grandmother died. To finish the job Sal started, I sneak children who need their colostomies reversed in through the rear door of the hospital. I fulfill my duty and heal the kids I can. But there is no end in sight to the flow of injured and traumatized children rushing through the hospital doors.

I write because I cannot sleep at night. Even if my words here are never read, I'm a step better for having let it out. I may not be making any difference being here with what I do and say, but the fact remains that I am here. I don't want these moments to be forgotten. The world should know. I see people live and die in this struggle, and even when they are gone forever it matters that they were here. I was here too. I saw it. I bore witness to these events; tragic, life-changing events for these unknown people in a hidden little corner of the world.

*Dec. 5, 2007*

A policeman who was shot in the penis told me that he wanted to be able to marry in the future. Once Kasim translated his words, I realized what he intended to say was that he was a virgin and wanted to be able to father a child. I was relieved at what the CT scan showed: the bullet had not entered his belly, and the artery in his leg was intact. I told the man, who was probably about twenty-two years old, that it looked like most of the tissue of his penis was alive, and I was hopeful that we wouldn't have to cut off much flesh. I smiled and tried to reassure him.

When urologist Noah and I brought him to the OR and started working on his injury, I realized I had been far too optimistic. It put me in a foul mood to see that under the small bullet holes in the skin, the base of the man's penis had been almost completely severed. The tube for his urine was uninjured, but it didn't seem like he had what he needed to ever have an erection again. It was questionable if most of his penis would even survive. I had foolishly opened my mouth before surgery, giving him a hope I wouldn't be able to back up. We didn't amputate anything, choosing instead to give the tissue a chance to recover on the slim chance it would survive. We shall see on subsequent operations.

Helicopters brought us four more patients who had been in the same car together. The driver told us a story. His cousin had been killed and the funeral had taken place that day. While driving from the burial site to a gathering of relatives, the man noticed a helicopter approaching from the side. Without warning or explanation the helicopter opened fire. His wife was shot through the leg in several places and bled to death on the way to the hospital. His niece had been shot through her breast and her abdomen. The man himself had a minor wound through his hand. I took care of his other cousin who had been shot through his neck and the small of his back.

As I operated, Kasim explained to me that people have become afraid to attend funerals. Any place that people gather together in Iraq is a liability. Sometimes people are too afraid to go to the morgue to claim the bodies of their slain relatives. Some will make sure, when they do risk the journey to a funeral, that women are seated up front where they are highly visible. Sometimes if the insurgents see women in the area, they will refrain from attacking. But you can never tell with terrorists. Travel is not yet safe.

The day brought us more patients. There was a fifteen-month-old girl with burns on her buttocks. Her wounds were washed and dressed. There was an elderly man who had been shot through his abdomen. As his cracked liver oozed blood, we struggled to restart his massively swollen, ailing heart with compressions and shocks. He bled out and died. Another one was shot in the head, and our neurosurgeon opened his skull to relieve the pressure. This afternoon I operated on a little girl who had been struck by fragments from an IED. Noah and I removed her kidney and stitched together her bleeding spleen with a square of mesh.

In the past three days, I've slept about four hours. This morning I stumbled and squinted through rounds in a bright blue scrub top decorated with Tweety Bird. My underwear had been sweat through from operating with a lead apron last night while helping one of the orthopedic surgeons drill pins to line up the broken shinbone of an Iraqi soldier. I didn't care too much about the two-day stubble sprouting around my chin. My throat was beginning to scratch with the cold that has been sweeping through the hospital staff. I headed back to the hooch for the three post-call S's.

*Dec. 7, 2007*

It is 2200, and we still have about five follow-up cases to do. Bones need to be aligned with metal pins and rods. Wounds need to be washed out and closed over drains. Our operation schedule got a little disrupted over the course of the day. Early this morning, there were two suicide bombings on the roads between here and Baghdad. One was a truck bomb, and the other was a female suicide bomber at a security checkpoint. The crew at the Forward Operating Base radioed our ER to tell us that there were as many as twenty inbound. We activated the MASCAL response. We called in all shifts of the hospital and congregated in the ED. Shortly thereafter, the first helicopter landed. The helipad crew rolled in with a skinny nine-year-old boy with a hole in his armpit and a drainage tube already placed between the ribs of his left chest. He was writhing in pain and drawing his legs to his chest. When we opened the valve on his chest tube, about two cups of bright red blood splashed out onto the floor. He still had good vital signs, but they would not last for long with that degree of blood loss. Portable X-rays confirmed that there was a metal fragment the size of a pencil eraser in his heart. Andy, the thoracic surgeon, and I quickly rolled him into OR1A.

All of our operating rooms were converted to double rooms with a second operating table brought in. We lifted the boy onto the table on the left and quickly slipped large catheters into his arteries, veins, and penis. Andy and I washed our hands. The tech prepped his entire chest and abdomen with a brown iodine solution. After throwing a cover of sterile blue sheets over his body, we incised the skin in the middle of his chest and used a small, battery-powered saw to cut his breast-plate in half. We hand-cranked the rib spreader, a device that works like a jack, to pry apart the cut edges of his sternum. Peering inside his chest, we cut into the thick white sac that holds the heart. We quickly found some clotted blood and sucked it out. The fragment had punctured the left side of the heart, traveled completely across the width of the organ, and lodged in the muscle just above the right ventricle. We could feel the sharp edges poking through the fatty lining as the muscle swelled and contracted rhythmically. It was incredibly fortunate the boy's blood had sealed the two holes in his heart, and he did not die minutes after injury. We used fine stitches like fishing line and patches of Teflon felt to repair the holes. The fragment was wedged in the delicate web of muscle in the meaty part of his heart, so we left it where it lay rather than risk causing more damage by removing it.

*Dec. 21, 2007*

Earlier this morning there was a USO Christmas concert featuring Kid Rock, Robin Williams, Lance Armstrong, Miss USA Rachel Smith, Lewis Black, and other intrepid celebrities visiting our base. The morning started out quite cold. I wished I had worn gloves as I walked into the hospital. By the time the show started, the sun had taken a little of the chill out of the air. Unfortunately, I missed the show because I was operating on the little boy who had been brought back to our hospital after a bout of intractable vomiting. A few of the surgeons made the show, and they said it was a good time. They were surprised to see Robin Williams join Kid Rock for one of his encores and accompany him on the harmonica. This entertainment crew is doing eight shows in six days. I'm sorry that I missed the concert, but I know I wouldn't have enjoyed it knowing the boy was waiting for me to start his surgery. A few of the wounded soldiers well enough to make the trip were bused to the stadium. I'm glad they got to see the show, but they'd be better off on a C-17 to Germany.

The hospital held a holiday party behind the CASF after the show. It was a chilly night, but that didn't stop just about every troop who wasn't on duty (and half who were) from showing up. We had a barbecue in a half-barrel with bratwurst from Germany and burgers from the DFAC. The party planning committee also ordered pizzas from the Pizza Hut, just down the street by the waste leeching pool. The tables were decorated with surgical sheets for tablecloths and lots of Christmas trinkets. We set up speakers and the karaoke machine.

We were shivering but kept returning to the grill for more to eat while the music played. After dinner, carolers who had been practicing since November favored us with "Silent Night" and "Gloria." Long after the cold had forced most back into the hospital, a few die-hards warmed the night with karaoke versions of "I'm Like a Bird" and "Lady Marmalade."

I've had my share of holidays apart from Meredith and the boys due to overnight call shifts. But a solitary holiday call night was different than being here. If I was lucky there wouldn't be too many traumas, and Meredith would bring the boys in so we could dine together. We would see what was being offered in the cafeteria, or Meredith would bring food from home in Tupperware containers for us to reheat in the call room microwave. The boys loved the novelty of cafeteria food. They enjoyed watching a video in the call room or climbing on the sculptures in the lobby. They would create murals on any available surface with dry erase markers. Even though I couldn't leave the hospital, it was a treat just to be together. The nurses would try to keep things quiet for a few hours so we could enjoy a protected moment together. After Meredith and the boys had left to go home, I felt like I could face any challenge through any sleepless night.

Here in Iraq, I have no visit from family. There is no hope of an eventual chance to go home to them after a thirty-six hour call shift is over. When I do get a chance to call home, I can't even depend on a reliable phone line.

Our Christmas celebration in Balad last night was a good opportunity to support each other and enjoy the holiday together. We all have the same longing for community, family, and the real life of home. But it seems like desperate subterfuge to try and convince ourselves it is fun and entertaining to spend a holiday away from our loved ones. Any conversation that goes beyond the most superficial "Merry Christmas" quickly turns into a competition to tell one another whom we would rather be with at that moment.

I sometimes wish I could simply unplug my mind and lie in a state of dormant sleep every moment I am not working. It would be so nice to just sleep the deployment away and wake up in January when the plane is waiting to take me home. Instead, I string myself along. Long nights of insomnia. Haunting the hospital, even when not on call, until I reach the point that sleep drops on me through the veil of my exhaustion.

## Dec. 29, 2007

One of our translators, Ali, is an American contractor employed by the US Army. He used to travel with a unit that patrolled outside the wire. He said Al Qaeda knew it was outgunned by US forces, so they adjusted their tactics. They would not directly engage US troops. They waited until soldiers had left an area, then attacked anyone who was in the open be they civilian or military. He said Al Qaeda attacked with continuous small arms fire and grenades. It seemed they were attacking in waves with one wave reloading while another was emptying their magazines on full auto. It was impossible for anyone to move while they were firing. Al Qaeda didn't care who they shot; men, women, and children were targeted equally. It was always hard to know when a barrage was coming because the Al Qaeda fighters wore the same garb as civilians. After the attack, those who were not neutralized would blend back into the population. I told him I was happy he was working in the hospital and no longer going outside the wire.

The assault today that brought us so many patients was directed against a concerned citizens' group. They had rejected Al Qaeda from their village and driven them out of their encampment in a neighboring area. As Al Qaeda fighters fled, a few rounded for a second sweep of the village. Our patients told the translator the Al Qaeda fighters opened fire on a crowded public area. There was no warning of the attack. They were shooting indiscriminately. The men told us they hit adults and children. We did not receive any children at the hospital. All the children shot in the village died on the scene.

Al Qaeda is not the only threat to the safety of civilians and children. I met one US Army captain who was embedded with the Iraqi Army as part of a training initiative. He spent several months training them and supervising raids.

He said they often used their firepower with a sense of panic. At the first sign these soldiers were under attack, they would all completely unload their weapons in a haphazard manner. Many of them would crouch down behind cover, such as a vehicle, then hold their weapons over their head and blindly spray bullets in the direction from which they thought they were being attacked. The captain, who had learned to take cover until the panicked troops had spent their ammunition, called this maneuver the Iraqi death blossom.

## Jan. 4, 2008

I was thirteen when I decided to become a doctor. I often babysat for neighbors and friends. I enjoyed caring for children. I thought that it would be very rewarding to take care of children as a pediatrician. Well, it turns out that caring for a sick child is a lot different than caring for a well child. It is extremely difficult to watch a child who is ill and suffering, and answer to worries of mothers and fathers. I have found that it is a lot easier taking care of an anesthetized child, which partly explains why I can survive a lot easier as a pediatric surgeon than a pediatrician. The things I do when I correct birth defects or surgical emergencies might seem violent or chaotic. But in the sterile calm of the operating room, isolated in the blue square of surgical towels, the careful cutting and controlled bleeding of a child isn't as frightening to me as seeing a wide-awake child in pain.

Still, medical care requires unpleasantness, and I find that I am often responsible for putting a child through misery on the path to getting well. I remember being a medical student assigned to the pediatric surgery service. During the day I assisted Dr. J. Alex Haller, a chair of pediatric surgery at Johns Hopkins, as he performed amazingly precise operations to transform a child's deformed and funnel-shaped chest into a healthy shape. The children drifted off to sleep at the beginning of the operation as they inhaled anesthetic gas perfumed with the scent of bubble gum or cherry. When the operation was over, they emerged from the anesthetic slowly and received strong narcotic pain medication.

During the night, I took call with residents and attended to the needs of the children staying on the pediatric surgery ward. The call would come; a child had lost his intravenous catheter and needed another. The resident on duty would send me to take care of it. By the time they called us, the nurses had already tried and failed. It always seemed absurd to me that I was being asked to try after a much more experienced nurse had been unable to complete the task. What I did have on my side was desperation. I wanted to become a pediatric surgeon more than anything in the world, and it seemed to me that I had to master this basic task if I was to have any hope of making it. Sure I could go back and wake up the intern if I failed, but at the moment it seemed that I was the last chance this child had to get a dearly needed IV catheter.

I can easily call up the pitiful scene in my mind. I would open the door to the procedure room and see the child, per-haps recovering from an appendectomy, or maybe dying from some cancer. She would have red-rimmed eyes and trails of tears down her cheeks from the previous attempts to insert a needle into a vein. The child's mother or father would be there, comforting her. They would turn and look to me, a

Posing on the steps of Johns Hopkins Hospital, May 1992. The white coat is given to medical students after the first year of medical school when we have our first duties caring for patients.

medical student, with eyes carrying a mixture of hope that I could help and suspicion that I could not.

Every time it went the same way. I introduced myself and explained that I was about to try again to insert an IV that would work for their child. I told the parents they were welcome to stay and watch whatever I did to their child, but if it were too difficult to endure, they could step outside for a moment. The nurse would help position the child and hold her arm down for me to work on. As soon as the child realized that another needle was coming, she would begin crying again. Some pleaded for me to stop; others screamed and yelled at their parents that they hated them. Either way, most parents began to cry. I hoped my needle would find its target on the first try and a deep red show of blood would appear at the hub of the needle. Often it didn't. Missing a vein would mean fresh cries from the child when I told the parent that I was very sorry but needed to try again. Thinking about it brings a lump to my throat even now. But I had desperation on my side. I knew that without that IV, we could not get that child well. No matter how much she cried or fought, it was unacceptable to give up and not give her the treatment she needed.

It felt horrible the first few times. After the IV was in I retreated to the stairwell, shaking, wondering if I could do this for a living. It got easier to start and easier to move on to the next task, but I still ache when I have to cause pain to an awake child. I never lie and say that it won't hurt.

*Jan. 6, 2008*

Demoralizing events occur, but we have to do our best, chin up, and hope for the best. Today, gunmen fired on a bus full of women and young girls. We received many of the injured. Some weren't lucky enough to make it to the hospital. One of the injured was pregnant. This wasn't her first brush with misfortune. She had delivered two other children, but one had died of a brain tumor. Her pregnancy was eight months along, but her husband had been killed seven months ago. Bullets and fragments of metal had pierced her hip and entered the tissue of her uterus. She lay on her side, in pain from the contractions stimulated by the injury. We gathered as much information on her baby as we could. How did the ultrasound look? What was the heart rate? We collected all the expert help we could find: an Army pediatrician across base in a sick call clinic, an OB nurse working on the ward. We called friends in Baghdad and back home for advice.

After heating up the operating room, we opened her belly and looked for damage caused by the bullet. The tissue of her uterus was bleeding and she was leaking urine from a gash in her bladder. I carefully opened her uterus, releasing the waters. I felt her baby's head and quickly unwound the umbilical cord from where it was wrapped around the neck. The baby slid smoothly from her womb. My partners, thoracic surgeon Andy and urologist Noah, helped cut the cord, and I brought the baby over to where Ruth, the Army pediatrician, was waiting with ER doc Julian. The baby was a beautifully formed boy, with rich brown hair. Covered in a waxy coating of vernix, his skin was a frighteningly purplish hue. We cleared his nasal passages of mucus, warmed him, jostled him, wiped him down, and pumped puffs of oxygen into his lungs until he drew breath and gave his first cry. With a stream of oxygen directed at his face, pink color spread across his skin. He let out a grunt. We bundled him in a makeshift incubator fashioned from a crib wrapped with food service cellophane and heated with a hose from a warm air blower. His mother required more work in the OR to control bleeding but was able to make it to the intensive care unit a short time later, heavily sedated and on life support.

The successful arrival of a baby was such a heartwarming and encouraging event in our little hospital. It seemed like nearly everyone drifted by to sneak a peek. The lucky bedside nurses got to feed him his first meal, which he took well. We fussed over his numbers and vital signs. We scowled over the threat of complications that might occur, and brainstormed stratagems to ward them off. He seemed to pay our worries no mind. I rushed back to my hooch to bring him a blue receiving blanket that Meredith had knit and sent with me to Iraq in case a baby might need to be warmed. His freshly cleaned, tiny features have been a calming precious beauty in our combat support hospital. If he can emerge safe from such a horrible event, perhaps there is hope for even better days to come.

A staff member securing the belongings of an injured Iraqi civilian holds a bloody bundle of Dinar notes in the ER of the 332nd Air Force Theater Hospital, January 2008.

*Jan. 10, 2008*

We were called to the ER to treat two trauma codes early this morning. The woman was moaning in pain and curled on one side to favor her right leg. Two bullets had hit her. One had ripped a chunk of flesh from the meat over her scapula, and the other had torn a hole through the inside surface of her thigh. A thin bridge of skin covered the wound in her thigh. When I looked through the hole, I could see through her leg to the bed beneath her.

The man who came with her had holes in all of his limbs. His skin was a lifeless purplish grey. The medics performed CPR the whole flight as they flew him to us. As soon as they had rolled his NATO gurney into the trauma bay, we took over the chest compressions and puffed oxygen into his lungs. We intubated him and made sure that his lungs weren't collapsed. We checked to see if his heart were leaking blood into the sac that surrounds it. We checked for any electrical activity with the electrocardiogram. We felt for pulses, listened for movement of air, and watched for any muscle reflexes. There were no signs of life. We stopped pushing on his chest and let him finish dying. In his pocket was a three-inch-thick stack of Iraqi 250 dinar bills, stained with his blood. They were locked away with his other belongings.

The woman he came in with has not yet regained consciousness. She was still sedated hours after her surgery. I don't know what the relationship is between them. When she is awake enough, one of us will tell her that her companion is dead.

Later in the day, several US troops were transported to our hospital. Their injuries resulted from an explosion. When they all arrived at once, our ER was flooded with personnel responding to the call for help. Patients had several doctors, nurses, and techs working on them. I even saw troops from other areas on base, Security Forces or flight line crew, volunteering their off-duty downtime to help an injured troop. Troops were quickly triaged and those who needed it were rushed off to the OR.

I spoke with one of the injured men while we were waiting for the CT scan machine to check his condition. He described the explosion to me. One of his friends had his legs broken by debris. He said, "His legs were twisted like spaghetti. They didn't even look like legs anymore, just some pounded meat coming out of the bottom of his body. It was the most disgusting thing I've ever seen."

I asked, "Who was that?"

"It was Badillo, Sir."

I was surprised to hear that it was the man two beds over, on whom I had just been working. I had splinted his legs, and I distinctly remember thinking that his legs looked great. I was relieved the breaks weren't as severe as most I see.

## Jan. 11, 2008

In Fallujah, a pregnant mother lay in the hospital for three days, and as best we can tell, her newborn contracted an infection during childbirth. He suffered seizures and difficulty breathing on his first day of life. The doctors there contacted our forces in the region. A helicopter medevac crew brought us this fragile, six-pound patient hoping we would save his life. His father rode in the helicopter with him, never leaving his side. When they arrived, we were able to resuscitate the baby and hook him up to a breathing machine. The father thanked me repeatedly for doing what I could for his boy. He also said what many other Iraqi's have said to me: "Thank you to each and every American soldier for leaving their home and risking their life to help Iraqi people."

Soon it became clear we could not keep his fragile newborn son alive for long. Even if we did, he would likely be crippled with brain damage, seizures, and cerebral palsy. The discussion I had with his father is one I've had before, but every time it is just as horrible. I told him that it was better the baby die gently than have us continue to force his little body to stay alive with machines. I told him if it were my boy, I wouldn't want him to go through it anymore. It rips my heart to even imagine it.

His father said, *"Shukran,"* and then more words I didn't understand.

Kasim told me, "He wants to thank you very much because you tried very hard to help. From the first day he was born, he didn't think there was any way his son could survive." This was emotionally difficult for Kasim to translate. I have taxed him too often with these weighty conversations. The father seemed to accept the dire situation much more peacefully than I could. He looked directly into my eyes and said, *"Ina lilahi wa-ina lilayhi innaa raji'un."*

Upon hearing this, Kasim dipped his head and muttered his assent in a hoarse whisper, *"Aywa."*

I asked Kasim, "What does it mean?"

"We belong to Allah, and to Allah we return. It is what we say when someone dies."

We removed the breathing tube and the child's chest became still. The father held his baby in his arms, rocking him gently, as he died.

*Jan. 12, 2008*

After dinner I wandered to the hospital to see if I could be of any use. In the long hallway leading to the ER I nearly collided with Kasim. He was dressed in a heavy jacket and carried a bulging, lightweight outdoorsman's backpack. He was laughing as he said, "Dr. Coppola, pardon me. I nearly knocked you over. I am sorry."

I helped him get his pack righted. "Kasim, what's going on?"

"It is so amazing I can barely even dare to believe it. My papers have come through and I have a visa to go to Jordan. I am leaving tonight. It was my friend in Iraqi Security Forces. Not only did he get my passport corrected, he arranged for me to get transportation to the airport. I'm flying out on a helicopter at 2200."

After congratulating him, I offered to walk him to the helipad, and then asked if he would make it to Jordan in time.

"Yes, yes, I have several days' leeway. Even better, I'm going to see her. She is meeting me in Amman. She will be there with her father. I am going to meet my future father-in-law! I am very nervous, but she told me not to worry."

"Just get there safely."

"It is good news that I have a flight all the way to Baghdad. I won't have to travel by land or risk the drive on route Irish."

I told him how thrilled I was.

"Your day to leave will come soon too. Did you ever think I would leave Iraq before you?"

"To be honest with you, I hoped you would." I didn't really know what to say to him. Standing before him in the deserted hallway, I realized there was a good chance I would never see him again. "Do you have everything you need? Food, do you need food for the trip?"

"No thank you, I have enough Gatorade and Pringles for three men. Thank you for everything Dr. Coppola."

"Kasim, I didn't do anything for you. I'm the one who should be thanking you for all the help you've been taking care of my patients. You've been such a great friend."

He thanked me again and went to check in for the flight at the staging area. Our Army liaison had him manifested to Baghdad, and then onto Baghdad International Airport.

"Goodbye Dr. Coppola. Perhaps I will see you in America."

"I'd like that very much."

He gave me the thumbs up and smiled without a worry on his face. He pushed open the door to the staging area and the chatter from the helicopter's rotors filled the air for a moment, before the door swung back shut on heavy springs. Through the tiny square window, I watched him turn and stride across Heroes Highway, a forty-foot-long canvas awning with an American flag stretched across it. Then he disappeared behind the concrete barrier where the Black Hawk was ready to fly him away.

*Jan. 13, 2008*

The other surgeons and I ride to family dinner together each night in the back of the Czar Car pickup truck. The sun sets before we head off on the two-mile trip to DFAC 3 across base. The landscape of Mesopotamia around us is a cold expanse of hard-packed ground with groves of scrubby eucalyptus and palm. The air is dry, and once the sun is down, the heat quickly flees the earth.

As the truck traverses the base, a brisk breeze flows over the cab. The wind penetrates my reflective Air Force T-shirt and bites my skinny frame, but I ride in the bed rather than the cab. The open breeze is a brief nightly reminder of cruising San Antonio with the top off the Wrangler and stars traveling overhead. Tonight the moon has yet to rise over the Tigris, but we see the evening star wink at us from the eastern horizon. Mars rises high, a luminous yellow-red speck ruling from afar.

The nightly circles we run over this small patch of ground summon memories of childhood in Madison, Connecticut. We spent our youth repeating the same circles in that small seaside town. At day's end, when the responsibility of schoolwork was done, or we had punched out of the kitchens and shops of summer jobs, we roamed the byways.

We didn't have the means to go far, and there weren't too many destinations to visit anyway. There was the Ben Franklin five-and-dime for candy or ice cream. We cut through the woods from Horsepond Road to the Highway 95 truck stop to play Space Invaders. Sometimes there was a pickup game of softball at the high school fields. But more often than not the destination was the beach.

Everyone made it to the beach at some point. I hung out with the other kids from my Catholic school and met up with the local public school kids to test my swagger. Some kids were lucky enough to own tiny Sunfish sailboats, and we would wade out to try and hitch a ride. Our parents had family cookouts at the town beach, and we roamed from table to table to see who had the best sodas and potato salad. Sometimes we crashed the dances at the private beach club where the rich kids were members. Late at night we skinny-dipped in the waves, daring each other to swim farther and farther out, where unseen buoys bobbed in oil-black water rippling with reflections from the moon.

We moved to the Connecticut shore when I was four years old, after my father had finished training as an obstetrician in Washington, DC. Across the years, I can see the yellow morning sun, low in the southeast, scattering diamonds of light across the Long Island Sound. In the air is the fishy smell of dead crabs in seaweed and the iodine scent of salt crystallized along the tide line.

Our swim instructor would toss us in the waves, and we basically learned by trying not to drown. The waves crashing on the Connecticut shore are little more than two foot ripples, but in my four-year-old eyes they loom as high, dark walls threatening to punish and drag me out to sea.

When I start to lose faith, I return to those days when seagulls would keen and cry overhead and waves would lift my feet from the stones and seaweed of the ocean floor. When I would bob in the current with a dizzy sensation of weightlessness, flailing my arms and holding my breath each time the tide broke in a foamy riot. Swept up and spun in the current, my body would scrape along the rocky bottom as sounds of life and seagulls disappeared underwater.

The ocean coughs me roughly upon the sandy shore. The wave slides back into the water to join its brothers. I am left on my hands and knees to hack out the taste of seaweed and spit the gritty sand forced into my throat. I rub the salty water from my eyelids, blink to see my mother waving at me. She sits cross-legged on her beach blanket, holding a paperback in one hand. Her brown hair fans in the breeze, and she wears big, round Jackie O sunglasses with tortoiseshell frames. In minutes the sun warms me and I leap to my feet, determined to master the water. My lungs flinch with tightness as I wade out past the point of comfort. I can't imagine any way I can survive another wave, but I swear I will try.

# Discussion Questions

1. There is a telling passage about Dr. Coppola's transformation at the start of the book when he shaves his head: "I feel a lot of things—loneliness, fear, concern for my family back in Texas. As the last vestiges of my stateside life pile in black-gray clumps on the wet earth, I take a full breath. No longer is there any doubt my part in this war is real" (page 12). Is Dr. Coppola someone who is ripe for such a transformation? Does he actively seek it out? Has anything similar happened in your own life?

2. In some ways, Dr. Coppola is portrayed as a classically heroic character; called to action, he must leave his home and overcome a series of difficult trials before finding redemption. Talk about how well Dr. Coppola matches your notion of the American hero—how do his habits, his interactions with people, the way he acts in traumatic situations, fit into or defy this notion. Is Dr. Coppola someone you'd like to get to know, work with, or have as a neighbor or a friend?

3. At the heart of the book lies a fundamental conflict between Dr. Coppola's duty as a healer, and his participation in a war he finds responsible for unnecessary deaths. Do you think this conflict is ever fully resolved in his mind? Does Dr. Coppola ever articulate a clear role for himself in Iraq?

4. Throughout the memoir the Iraqi translators serve an important role, allowing Dr. Coppola to communicate with sick and injured Iraqi patients in the hospital. What do you think of his decision to disregard military restrictions to visit their tent? What does Dr. Coppola learn about the translators as he crosses this boundary?

5. The book is divided into three major sections: Dr. Coppola's first deployment to Balad Air Base, his life at home in San Antonio, and his second deployment—this time to a newly expanded and modernized Balad Air Base. Did you notice changes within Chris's character as he moved from one location to the next? Have you ever had the experience of traveling some place new and feeling an altered sense of self?

6. After the democratically-held Iraqi elections in January of 2005, Dr. Coppola expresses a cautious optimism about the future of the country: "There is good being done here today. The Iraqi people are stepping up to the plate and voting. They are voting for a better future for themselves and their children. For decades Iraqis suffered under the reign of Saddam Hussein, a sadistic monster who institutionalized rape, torture, and murder to tighten his stranglehold on the country. When Kurds in northern Iraq rose in defiance, he killed them indiscriminately with poison gas: man, woman, and child. But today the injured entering our doorway raise their ink-stained fingers in a gesture of victory" (page 41). Discuss your reaction to the risks many Iraqi civilians took to vote. Are the casualties many Iraqi's suffered a painful but natural part of attaining democracy? Would you take similar risks to vote in your own country?

7. As a U.S. military surgeon at a combat support hospital, Dr. Coppola's first responsibility is to combat troops injured in the field. However, in treating infants Farrah and Leila, Dr. Coppola makes decisions to prioritize their care, at times soliciting the participation of other staff members. Do you think Dr. Coppola was justified in doing so? How do fellow U.S. military surgeons and nurses react to his desire to provide care for Iraqi children? Do you think Dr. Coppola's wish to assign a pediatric surgeon to all U.S. combat support hospitals during wartime is justified?

8. Early in the memoir, Dr. Coppola is stricken by the death of female National Guardswoman: "I've treated many women who have suffered non-combat trauma before. Some made it, some did not. But I cannot wrap my mind around the cold reality of a woman being killed at war" (page 34). Discuss your reaction to Dr. Coppola's distinction between the death of women and the death of men in war. Do Western ideals about gender equality apply in the context of war? Based on what you know about his character, why do you think this death feels so different to Chris?

9. Dr. Coppola describes how leisure and recreation provide an important outlet for troops during deployment. Were you surprised by the various types of recreational opportunities available on the base such as the Sustainer movie theater, the gym, and the swimming pool? How do Dr. Coppola's own personal hobbies—gardening, mountain bike riding, and writing—distinguish him from other troops?

10. With the inauguration of the Surge in 2007, President George Bush ordered the deployment of more than 20,000 U.S. soldiers, and extended the tours of 4,000 Marines, to provide additional security to Baghdad and the Al Anbar Province. Trauma Surgeon Sal suggests the Surge has been beneficial for U.S. troops but has inspired a countervailing effect on Iraqi's: "Now that Al Qaeda can't get to the troops easily, they've been targeting civilians. It's frightening" (page 203). What are your reactions to this statement? Looking back, do you think the Surge was the right decision?

11. As an accomplished, middle-aged surgeon who has completed humanitarian missions in Haiti and Brazil, Dr. Coppola may not fit the typical depiction of a U.S. soldier represented in popular media. Did any of the other surgeons Chris describes change your views toward the culture, professional backgrounds, and belief systems of those in U.S. military? Did you find any differences between Chris's depiction of military surgeons and combat troops?

12. In writing this book, Dr. Coppola chose to preserve, almost verbatim, the original language of "Sad News" (pages 99-100), one of many letters he wrote to his wife and children during his first deployment. Do you notice any differences in the style and tone of this letter from the other chapters in the book? More generally, how does the form and style of this memoir compare to others you have read?

13. Much of the book is about Dr. Coppola's personal and psychological struggle to straddle the worlds separating his military family from his family in San Antonio, Texas. Discuss how well Chris was able to balance these dual obligations.

14. Did the book change your views toward Islam or Muslims? Consider Dr. Coppola's frank assertion that "the Muslims I meet every day seem just like me, people more concerned about the health and happiness of their families than any holy war" (page 91). Discuss this statement in the context of Chris's own conflicted feelings about his religious beliefs.

15. Descriptions of the blood and gore inside the surgery room are often explicit and colloquial. "I take out a set of shears, exactly like the one I keep in my kitchen to quarter chickens, and cut off his leg with two snips" (page 96). Did this level of detail add to your experience of the book? Did it have a different emotional effect when it was used in descriptions of children? In your opinion, how would the book have read differently, if Dr. Coppola had maintained more detachment from the surgical procedures?

# Appendix A

## "Children Treated at an Expeditionary Military Hospital in Balad"

Abstract and Comment by Lt. Col. Chris Coppola, Maj. Brian Leninger, Lt. Col. Todd Rasmussen, and Col. David Smith. Originally published in Archives of *Pediatric and Adolescent Medicine* (Volume 160, 2006). Copyright © 2006 American Medical Association. All rights reserved.

---

## ARTICLE

# Children Treated at an Expeditionary Military Hospital in Iraq

*Lt Col Christopher P. Coppola, USAF, MC; Maj Brian E. Leininger, USAF, MC; Lt Col Todd E. Rasmussen, USAF, MC; Col David L. Smith, USAF, MC*

**Objective:** To describe the treatment of children at an expeditionary military hospital in wartime Iraq.

**Design:** Descriptive, retrospective study.

**Setting:** The 332nd Air Force Theater Hospital in Balad, Iraq, January 1, 2004, to May 31, 2005.

**Patients:** All 85 children (of 1626 total patients) evaluated and treated at the hospital during the study period.

**Interventions:** Indicated surgical procedures performed on children.

**Main Outcome Measures:** Age, sex, diagnosis, injury, operations, and complications for children during the study period.

**Results:** The 85 children (age range, 1 to 17 years; mean, 8 years) represents 5.2% of all patients. Thirty-four (61%) of the 56 children for whom sex was recorded were male. Injury was the diagnosis for 48 children (56%). Of these, the cause was fragmentation wound in 25 children (52%), penetrating trauma in 11 (23%), burn in 9 (19%), and blunt trauma in 3 (6%). The site of injury was the lower extremity in 18 children (38%), head in 11 (23%), upper extremity in 8 (17%), abdomen in 8 (17%), and chest in 3 (6%). Nontraumatic conditions has congenital, infectious, gastrointestinal, and neoplastic causes. During the study, 134 operations were performed on 63 children. There were 5 deaths.

**Conclusions:** Expeditionary military hospitals will encounter both injured and noninjured children seeking medical care. To optimize the care of these children, it will be necessary to provide the proper personnel, training, and equipment.

*Archives of Pediatric and Adolescent Medicine* 2006; Vol. 160: pgs 972-976.

---

## COMMENT

This report describes the care of children by an expeditionary hospital in Iraq. Our primary mission as a level III hospital was to provide evaluation, resuscitation, and surgical care to combat-injured troops. When stabilized, American troops were evacuated to the regional medical center in Germany. However, our facility experienced "mission creep" because of the presence of injured civilians, including children. Children additionally had dehydration and malnutrition, which contribute to increase mortality. After January 1, 2005, a pediatric surgeon was available and a broader range of nontraumatic conditions were treated in children.

Our experience mirrors that of other military medical providers in Afghanistan and Iraq in that fragmentation of blast injuries were the most common mechanisms of injury. This is the typical pattern of injury in victims of improvised explosive devices and suicide bombers. Children are particularly vulnerable to unexploded ordnance and land mines. Blast and fragmentation devices produce multiple injuries over different regions of the body. This is especially true in civilians, who lack the body armor worn by combatants. The injuries are a combination of penetration and crush of the soft tissues, often accompanied by fractures. The wounds are contaminated by fragments of the explosive device, vehicle shrapnel, clothing, and dirt. This requires extensive debridement and high-pressure irrigation to clear the wounds of debris and devitalized tissue. The fragments from improvised explosive devices and land mines produce a cone of injury larger than the entry wound. Injured children at our facility required multiple procedures for debridement of necrotic tissue, which delayed primary closure of the wounds.

The lower extremity was the most common site of injury, followed by the head. This differs from reports of injured adults, who sustain upper and lower extremity injuries more often than head injuries. This patern may differ in children owing to their shorter stature and the proportionately larger size of the head. These factors make the head a more likely target of fragmentation devices. The third most common operation performed, after soft tissue wound operations and fracture fixation, was craniotomy for head injury.

Nontraumatic conditions were treated at our facility. Some children were referred by Iraqi institutions unable to provide the acuity of care required. Others chose to seek care at the American military base bacause of financial hardship, another family member being treated at our hospital, or referral after an encounter with American soldiers. Through the initiative and innovation of the hospital personnel, we were able to make the most of the austere conditions and limited resources, and we

optimized the care provided for these children.

Some deficiencies in resources became manifest. There was a short supply of the smallest endotracheal tubes, sizes 3.5 to 5.0. Twenty-two– and 24-gauge catheters were quickly depleted following intravenous access in the hands of providers not accustomed to pediatric care. Finally, personnel experienced in pediatric anesthesiology, critical care, and critical care nursing were rare in our facility. The few individuals with this experience were often hard-pressed to cover prolonged periods when extremely ill children were present in the hospital.

Military pediatric specialists were dispersed throughout the theater of combat, assigned responsibilities for adult combat troops. Once we discovered their presence, these providers represented a valuable resource for the care of children. This pool of pediatric expertise was also present during the first Gulf War. On one occasion, a pediatric anesthesiologist, who was assigned north of our location, traveled to our base to anesthetize a child for portoenterostomy. One pediatrician, officially assigned as the battalion surgeon for helicopter personnel on our base, participated in our weekly clinic. Another example of pooled resources was the case of the 2-year-old girl who underwent resection of a cervical cystic hygroma at our hospital and later received radiofrequency ablation treatment of her enlarged tonge at a different combat support hospital.

Our experiences have demonstrated several important lessons in the care of children in a ware zone. Any hospital near conflict should expect to receive civilian casualties, including children. The most common machanism of injury in children is fragmentation injury, and the most common sites are the lower extremity and head. Fragmentation injuries are contaminated, resulting in necrotic tissue and requiring careful and repeated debridement. The neuro-

surgeons assigned to the facility were
surprised by the excellent outcomes
after penetrating head trauma in this
setting. Local health resources may be
so disrupted that children cannot be
safely discharged until they are well
enough to survive under the care of
their families. To provide adequate care
for children during war, expeditionary
medical hospitals must prepare for
them by providing the proper personnel,
training, and equipment.

# Appendix B

## Military and Medical Acronyms

| | |
|---|---|
| ABU | airman battle uniform |
| AFN | Armed Forces Network |
| Airevac | air evacuation |
| AOD | anesthesiologist on duty |
| AOR | Area of Responsibility |
| ATV | all-terrain vehicle |
| BDU | battle dress uniform |
| BIAP | Baghdad International Airport |
| BKA | below the knee amputation |
| BMT | basic military trainee |
| BX | Base Exchange |
| CONEX | container express |
| CPR | cardiopulmonary resuscitation |
| CSH | combat support hospital |
| CT | computed tomography |
| DCU | desert camouflage uniform |
| DFAC | dining hall |
| DIC | disseminated intravascular coagulation |
| DSN | defense switched network |
| ECMO | extra-corporeal membrane oxygenation |
| EKG | electrocardiogram |

| | |
|---|---|
| ENT | ear, nose, and throat |
| ER | emergency room |
| GSW | gunshot wound |
| HMMWV | High Mobility Multipurpose Wheeled Vehicle |
| HR | human remains |
| IBA | individual body armor |
| ICP | intracranial pressure |
| ICU | intensive care unit |
| IED | improvised explosive device |
| IV | intravenous |
| KBR | Kellogg, Brown, and Root |
| MASCAL | mass casualty |
| MiG | Mikoyan-Gurevich |
| MRAP | Mine Resistant Ambush Protected (Vehicle) |
| MRE | Meal, Ready-to-Eat |
| MRI | magnetic resonance imaging |
| MURT | medical unit readiness training |
| MWR | moral, welfare, and recreation |
| NATO | North Atlantic Treaty Organization |
| NVG | night vision goggles |
| OB/GYN | obstetrician/gynecologist |
| OIF | Operation Iraqi Freedom |
| OR | operating room |
| PA | physician's assistant |
| PACHOD | pan-coated chocolate disc |
| PAD | patient administration division |
| Perfed | perforated |
| PICU | pediatric intensive care unit |
| PJ | pararescue jumper |
| PLX | pharmacy, laboratory, and x-ray |
| PTSD | post-traumatic stress disorder |
| PTU | physical training uniform |

PX          Post Exchange
RPG         rocket-propelled grenade
RT          respiratory technician
SOD         surgeon on duty
USO         United Service Organization
VBIED       vehicle borne improvised explosive device
WHMC        Wilford Hall Medical Center

ML $^{12}/_{10}$